BASEBALL
And The Color Line

D0285060

BaseBall
And The Color Line

by Tom Gilbert

The African-American Experience
FRANKLIN WATTS
New York ○ Chicago ○ London ○ Toronto ○ Sydney

*Frontispiece: Satchel Paige, left;
Jackie Robinson, right.*

Photographs copyright ©: National Baseball Hall of Fame, Inc.,
Cooperstown, N.Y.: pp. 2, 124, 130, 138, 142, 149; National
Baseball Library, Cooperstown, N.Y.: pp. 15, 32, 40, 51, 61, 71,
77, 98, 114, 116, 118, 123, 155; Negro Leagues Baseball
Museum, Inc.: p. 102

Library of Congress Cataloging-in-Publication Data

Gilbert, Thomas W.
Baseball and the color line/by Tom Gilbert.
p. cm.—(The African-American experience)
Includes bibliographical references (p.   ) and index.
ISBN 0-531-11206-3 (lib. bdg.) — ISBN 0-531-15747-4 (pbk.)
1. Afro-American baseball players—History. 2. Baseball—United
States—History. I. Title. II. Series
GV863.A1G57 1995
796.357'0973—dc20   94-23935
                                                             CIP AC

Copyright © 1995 by Tom Gilbert
All rights reserved
Printed in tℎe United States of America
6 5 4 3 2 1

CONTENTS

BASEBALL
And The Color Line

GENTLEMAN'S AGREEMENT

African Americans and Baseball's Beginnings

The baseball color line ended in 1946. That was the year the Brooklyn Dodgers signed Jackie Robinson to play with its Montreal farm club. The following season he came up to the major leagues. Formerly a shortstop in the Negro Leagues, Robinson became the first African American to play in the minor or major leagues in the twentieth century.

As long as most people could remember, American professional baseball had been segregated: the Negro Leagues were for African Americans and the white leagues, or organized baseball, were for white players. Robinson's arrival meant the end of this system. Most of the other major-league team owners of the time favored keeping baseball segregated. But after 1947 they had to follow suit and sign other Negro Leaguers if they wanted to stay competitive. By 1959, every major league team had fielded at least one African-American player and the Negro Leagues were virtually out of business. Today, baseball is completely integrated on the field level. Roughly one-quarter of all players in the majors are African Americans.

Baseball integrated itself peacefully and voluntarily. It would be difficult to overestimate what a great blow this was against racial segregation, or "Jim Crow," (laws and customs that separated the races), in all walks of American life. Baseball was the nation's oldest and most important professional sport; it was the only one to be called the "national pastime." Professional baseball had been strictly segregated since the nineteenth century. If baseball could change, Americans began to wonder, then why not the rest of society?

Soon after Jackie Robinson joined the Brooklyn Dodgers, pressure grew on schools, legislatures, the armed forces, and other American institutions to stop practicing racial discrimination. The sight of African Americans and white Americans playing side-by-side on major league baseball fields set a positive example for the country and helped build momentum for the civil rights movement of the 1950s and 1960s. Without Jackie Robinson and the integration of baseball, the struggles for racial equality during those years might have turned out very differently.

The Robinson episode, however, was not the first time baseball and the issue of race in America had come together. The story of the color line ended in 1947, but it had a beginning and a middle as well. From the start of the game in the early nineteenth century until today, baseball's racial attitudes have mirrored those of society. To understand the history of race relations in baseball is to better understand the history of race in America.

To find the beginning of the story of baseball and the color line, you have to go back to the first half of the nineteenth century, before the Civil War, when in a few northeastern cities baseball was changing from a casual children's pastime into a more serious sport played by adults. This was also a time of great

*The New York Knickerbockers, the first
baseball club, played the first baseball match
under modern rules in 1846.*

national soul searching over slavery and racism; what
to do about African-American slavery was the
number-one political issue. The problem of race
touched everything, even the young game of baseball.

The early baseball clubs were founded by groups
of middle-class young men from New York City and
Brooklyn during the 1840s and 1850s. Some of these
young men may well have been believers in the abolitionist cause. At that time slavery was completely
illegal in New York, as in all of the other fourteen
Northern states. The vast majority of African
Americans, however, lived in the South—where slavery was legal. Many white Americans of this time

began to feel that slavery ought to be eliminated in the South, too. A great wave of antislavery sentiment rose up. Two of the most conspicuous expressions of that sentiment were the colonialist movement, which sought to return African Americans to Africa, and the abolitionist movement, which campaigned for freedom and civil rights for African Americans in this country. As abolitionism grew, it caused more and more tension between the North and the South. Abolitionists helped operate the Underground Railroad, a secret network that helped slaves escape to freedom in the North.

The early baseball clubs were founded on the model of English amateur athletic clubs. These clubs were more like today's athletic or country clubs than modern sports franchises. "Gentlemanly" behavior was strictly enforced. The New York Knickerbockers, the first baseball club, fined its members for swearing at the umpire. Baseball in the early days was largely a friendly social event; competition among clubs in preparing the postgame banquet was at least as intense as that of the ball game itself. And it was strictly amateur; there were no paid players.

Baseball—and abolitionism—gained popularity throughout the East and Midwest during the early 1850s, when America was increasingly becoming divided over the question of whether slavery should be allowed in such new states as Texas, Oregon, and California. With more and more Americans playing baseball, the pressures of competition among clubs, cities, and regions inevitably were leading to a gradual breakdown of amateurism; clubs recruited the best available talent regardless of class, social, or geographic considerations. Organizations of shipyard workers or volunteer fire fighters fielded teams that equaled or surpassed those of the white-collar workers who had founded the sport. Top players, particularly pitchers, enticed by offers of a job or money under the table, began to jump from team to team and city to city. The beginning of the era of organized, professional leagues was around the corner.

By 1858—the year that Abraham Lincoln delivered his famous speech warning of the dangers of tolerating slavery, a speech which included the line "A house divided against itself cannot stand"—the first national baseball organization had been formed. It was called the National Association of Base Ball Players, or NABBP. Although this organization was the forerunner of today's organized professional baseball leagues, it was not a league in the modern sense. At its annual convention, the NABBP would publish an official set of baseball rules and set admission standards for member clubs, but it did not schedule games, award championships, or negotiate with players. Like the first baseball clubs, the NABBP was completely amateur.

NABBP membership records tell the story of the wildfire spread of the sport throughout the Northern, Midwestern and Middle Atlantic states. Sixteen member clubs were represented at the convention of 1858; later that year thirteen more were added. Forty-nine clubs attended the NABBP convention in 1859, a year that saw radical abolitionist John Brown seize the federal arsenal at Harpers Ferry, West Virginia. Brown's hopes of sparking a slave rebellion in Virginia were ended by his capture and hanging. There were sixty-two member clubs in 1860, the year that South Carolina seceded from the United States and made the Civil War inevitable. Even though barely a decade had passed since the New York Knickerbockers had played the first baseball match under modern rules, in 1846, and the game was only just beginning to spread south of Washington, D.C., baseball had established itself as America's game. It was already being regarded as an important national institution. Newspaper reporters of the late 1850s wrapped base- ball in the American flag, praising it for embodying American virtues such as fairness, resourcefulness, and courage. By 1860, calling baseball the "national pastime" was already a cliché.

Unfortunately, these early Northern baseball clubs participated in another American national pastime as well—racism. Every single club in the NABBP restricted membership to whites only, and many other white clubs of that time are known to have had ex- plicit policies—or, more typically, unwritten so-called "gentleman's agreements"—that excluded African Americans.

Little is recorded about African-American baseball before the Civil War. There are scattered references in contemporary newspapers to Brooklyn-based African- American baseball clubs named the Unknowns, Monitors, and Colored Unions. Philadelphia was also home to several African-American clubs. Both Brooklyn and Philadelphia had well-established African-American communities with a middle class that could support amateur sporting clubs along the lines of the early white clubs. It is ironic that the foundation for the baseball color line was laid in the same Northern cities and in the same Northern states whose antislavery activism provoked the South into secession and caused the great Civil War. The North may have been free of slavery in the years leading up to the Civil War, and Northerners may have opposed slavery and racism as practiced hundreds of miles away in the South, but in Boston, Philadelphia, or New York, they didn't always practice what they preached. Free African Americans in those cities could not escape Jim Crow or his "more slick, more sophisti- cated" cousin, James Crow, historian Harold Seymour's

*This drawing depicts Union prisoners of war
playing baseball in a Confederate camp in
Salisbury, North Carolina. One team is mainly
composed of New Yorkers.*

term for the subtler type of discrimination practiced
in the North.

Many baseball clubs disbanded or stopped play
ing during the Civil War years, from 1861 to 1865
But the war may have actually helped spread the
game throughout the North and South by mixing
together soldiers from such baseball hotbeds as New
York City with men from other states. There are written accounts, photographs, and drawings that tell of
wartime baseball matches, some watched by immense
crowds, in Southern prison camps and Union camp-
grounds in the South. On Christmas Day 1862, for

instance, a New York unit called Duryea's Zoaves played an all-star team representing the rest of the Union army at Hilton Head, South Carolina, before a crowd estimated by one witness at 40,000—easily the largest baseball crowd in history up to that time. Many Southerners, both white and African-American, got their first exposure to baseball as a serious adult sport at such events—or, if the stories can be believed, when Southern soldiers played against Northern soldiers under white flags during lulls in the fighting.

Many professional baseball players of the 1870s and 1880s, such as National League superstars Cap Anson from Iowa and Al Spalding from Illinois, remembered learning the game as boys from returning Civil War veterans. To Spalding, who wrote a history of baseball in 1911, the game played a part in healing the bitterness of the postwar period. "It was during the Civil War," Spalding writes, "that the game of baseball became our national game; for against it there was no prejudice—North or South; and from that day to this it has been played with equal fervor and equal prowess in every section of our beloved country."[1]

The end of the war brought on a second baseball boom. Ninety-one clubs attended the 1865 NABBP convention. In 1866 the nation's fans eagerly followed an exciting best-two-out-of-three series, billed as deciding the national championship, which was played by the Brooklyn Atlantics and the Philadelphia Athletics. A crowd of over 25,000 rowdy fans swarmed onto the field and forced cancellation of game one in Philadelphia. More than 15,000 paid to see the rescheduled game at Brooklyn's Capitoline Grounds. All the commotion and excitement caused one newspaper reporter to wonder if baseball were just a fad that was "about played out." NABBP records of 1866 show, however, that the sport was continuing to expand to the West and South. There were now 202 member clubs, and although three-fourths of them were concentrated in New York, New Jersey, Pennsylvania, and Connecticut, there were ten clubs from Washington, D.C.; five from Maryland; two each from Iowa, Tennessee, Mississippi, and Kansas; and one each from Virginia, Kentucky, and Oregon.

The end of the Civil War also brought one of the most turbulent periods in race relations in American history. The victorious Union army remained in the South until 1877, twelve years after General Robert E. Lee's surrender at Appomattox. The Union army's mission was to implement a radical program of reform, much of it aimed at improving the status and guaranteeing the newly-won civil rights of former slaves, who had been set free by President Abraham Lincoln's Emancipation Proclamation of 1863 and a number of Constitutional amendments. At first the reform program, which became known as Reconstruction, inspired great optimism among Northern abolitionists and African Americans everywhere. In 1865 Congress established the Freedmen's Bureau to fund educational programs for African-American ex-slaves and passed the Thirteenth Amendment to the United States Constitution, which outlawed slavery everywhere in the country. The following year, Congress enacted the Civil Rights Act, which granted full citizenship rights to all those born in the United States, except for Native Americans. Even though it did not specifically exclude women, many of the provisions of the Civil Rights Act—and many of the provisions of the other laws and amendments that were passed as part of Reconstruction— were not, in practice, applied to women. Even after the ratification of the Fourteenth and Fifteenth Amendments, for example, most states did not allow women to vote. In 1868 Congress passed the

Fourteenth Amendment to the Constitution after realizing the Civil Rights Act was insufficient to guarantee citizenship and voting rights to African Americans. Freed slaves were led to believe that Congress would break up the big Southern plantations and provide each of them with "forty acres and a mule" as a reparation payment for their suffering under slavery and as an economic stake in the new, racially-reconstructed Southern society.

Reconstruction was hampered from the beginning, however, by political divisions in Washington, D.C., and in the Northern states. Much of the reform legislation was enacted by Congress over strong opposition, including that of President Andrew Johnson of Tennessee. Johnson, who became president after Lincoln's assassination in April of 1865, vetoed the Freedmen's Bureau Bill, the Civil Rights Act, and even a bill granting African Americans the right to vote in the District of Columbia. In each case Reconstructionists in Congress, led by Pennsylvania's Thaddeus Stevens, had to put together the two-thirds majority necessary to override a presidential veto. And from the very beginning, Reconstruction policies encountered a powerful backlash in the South. White Southerners bitterly resented the prolonged presence of Northern soldiers on their soil. They hated even more the civilian officials who came down from the North to administer and enforce Reconstruction programs; these officials they scornfully referred to as "carpetbaggers." The racist Ku Klux Klan was founded in Tennessee in 1865; its purpose was to deny African-American citizens their rights and to sabotage Reconstruction.

Judging from a number of measures passed by Congress in 1866, 1867, and 1868, the Klan's efforts had some effect. The New Freedmen's Bureau Bill subjected to military trials—and, sometimes, hanging—those who tried to deprive African Americans of their citizenship rights. The First, Second, Third, and Fourth Reconstruction Acts responded to widespread intimidation of African-American voters by imposing martial law on the Southern states. The Reconstruction Acts required that the Union army take the place of the local government until those states ratified the Fourteenth and the Fifteenth Amendments, which required that all citizens receive the "equal protection of the law" and that no state deny or abridge the right to vote based on "race, color, or previous condition of servitude."

In the end, Reconstruction was a mixed success. Though exhausted by the fight against the Klan and the Northern political enemies of Reconstruction, Congress did manage to bully the South into granting African-Americans the right to register and vote. Not only did the African-American vote make up General Ulysses S. Grant's entire margin of victory in the presidential election of 1869, but it also elected African Americans to Congress and the Senate for the first time in American history: Senator Hiram Revels of Mississippi and Representative J. H. Rainey of South Carolina.

Reconstruction had its failures, too. Relations between North and South were polarized, fueling a white supremacist movement that would come back to haunt American history in the late nineteenth century and well into the twentieth. Reconstruction failed to fulfill all the expectations it had created among African Americans in the North and in the South. The descendants of the slaves are still waiting for their forty acres and a mule. Hard economic times and persecution by the KKK led thousands of former slaves to migrate to the North, where many were disappointed to find that there was no escape from racism and discrimination there, either. While race relations up North seemed smoother on the surface, this African-American influx caused a growing uneasiness. Many of the same Northerners who had recently fought to free the Southern slaves discovered that they did not wish to work alongside, live nearby, or ride in the same streetcar with free African Americans.

Those who hoped that the combination of the Northern victory in the Civil War and Reconstruction might mean a quick end to the color line in baseball were also soon to be disappointed. Thanks to papers discovered a few years ago by baseball historian Harold Seymour, we know in detail the story of how the African-American Pythian Base Ball Club of Philadelphia tried to join the National Association of Base Ball Players and was rejected because of race. The Pythians belonged to a solidly middle-class African-American fraternal organization, the Knights of Pythias, which had been founded in Washington, D.C., in 1864. The Philadelphia chapter boasted a number of members who were prominent figures in the African-American community. These included William Still, who led the successful battle to integrate Philadelphia's streetcar system in 1866, and Octavius Catto, a respected soldier, teacher, and athlete whose shooting by a white man in 1871 led to a race riot.

The sad thing about this episode is how similar in every way the Pythian club was to all-white baseball clubs of the time. Its constitution enforced a moral code at least as strict as that of the New York Knickerbockers, requiring that members refrain from gambling, foul language, and hard liquor. Club records show the same devotion to amateurism and lavish hospitality found in similar white organizations. After a game against a team of African-American federal employees, the Mutuals of Washington, D.C., the Pythians laid out a spread of wine, assorted meats, cheese, ice cream, and cigars for their opponents and guests. The club may have played informally against white teams at this time; the Pythians are known to have shared a friendly relationship, as well as playing facilities and umpires, with the Athletics, a nationally-famous white club. After an official of the Pythians congratulated the Athletics for "upholding the pride of Philadelphia" in an 1868 contest, the Athletics publicly thanked the African-American club for "these manifestations of confidence from our brethren in the city."[2]

None of this friendliness seems to have mattered, however, when, in 1867, the Pythians sent a delegate to apply for membership in the Pennsylvania chapter of the NABBP at its annual convention in Harrisburg. The NABBP's response was a case study in Northern queasiness and conflicted emotions in racial matters. In the morning of the opening day of the convention, white delegates begged the Pythian delegate, R.S. Bun, to withdraw his application in order to spare the association the embarrassment of turning it down for racial reasons; Bun declined. The association leadership then spent the afternoon attempting to stall the motion by a series of parliamentary maneuvers, but these were stymied by white delegates who supported the African-American club. A vote was scheduled for later that evening, but when it became apparent that the vote would go against the Pythians, a group of white delegates—including some who had argued for the Pythians' admission—finally persuaded Bun to give up. In his report back to Philadelphia, Bun wrote that the white baseball men "seemed disposed to show their sympathy and respect for our club by showing every possible courtesy and kindness."[3] They even paid Bun's train fare home.

This story illustrates a fundamental fact about Northern racial discrimination in general and the baseball color line in particular: the whites who enforced it were reluctant to do so openly or on the record because they knew that it was wrong. This is evident in the baseball world's somewhat guilty reaction to an NABBP report that was issued to member clubs as a result of the Pythian affair. "It is not presumed by your committee," the report reads, "that any club who have [sic] applied are composed of persons of color, or any portion of them; and the recommendations of your committee are based upon this view, and they unanimously report against the admission of any club which may be composed of one or more colored persons." According to contemporary baseball authority Henry Chadwick, the object of this report was to "keep out of the convention the discussion of any subject having a political bearing." An 1868 official baseball guide offers the rationalization that the report was passed "in the belief that if colored clubs were admitted there would be in all probability some division of feeling, whereas, by excluding them no injury could result to anybody, and the possibility of any rupture being created on political grounds would be avoided"—as though the exclusion of players and clubs because of race was a question of etiquette rather than one of morality.

That is the last official statement on racial exclusion in baseball during the late 1860s. After the rejection of the Pythians, African-American baseball players put their efforts into developing teams along separate lines. New African-American clubs sprang up throughout the East and Midwest and such older ones as the Pythians prospered. Octavius Catto's old club survived to be a founding member of the League of Colored Baseball Clubs, one of the first African-American leagues, in 1887.

Not that occasional matches between white and African-American clubs did not still occur. In September 1869 the Pythians played what was billed as the first formal "mixed" match, against the City Items, a white team sponsored by the *Philadelphia City Item* newspaper. The Pythians won, 27–17. A week or two afterward, they faced the Washington Olympics, a national power among white clubs, and lost by 44–23. In a time like this, when scores in the high double figures or even triple figures were common, to lose 44–23 to a top club was no embarrassment. It would be the equivalent of a score of 7–3 or 9–5 in today's game. Later that same Fall, another African-American team, the Alerts, also issued a challenge to the Olympics. Despite objections from "officious parties" [anti-Reconstruction politicians or NABBP officials, perhaps], the Olympics accepted—vowing, in General Grant's famous phrase from the Civil War, "to fight it out on this line." In an account drawn from contemporary newspaper coverage, one historian gives this description of the colorful scene:

> The match drew a large "concourse of friends of both" numbering about 5,000, on September 20th. The Alerts were nicely uniformed in dark gray shirts, black pants and caps. The Olympics wore their new uniforms of white flannel shirt and pants, a blue cord down the pants leg with buckle just below the knee, light blue stockings, a white skull cap trimmed with blue cord, blue belt, and old English letter "U" on the breast of the shirt. The Alerts looked sharp in practice but collapsed in the game. Olympics, 55; Alerts, 4 (7 innings).[4]

Shortly after this match, the African-American Mutuals, old opponents of the Pythians, made a better showing against the Olympics, losing 24–15.

In spite of the success of such interracial events, no African-American player or club after the Pythians tested the baseball color line by trying to join the NABBP. Baseball moved on to another controversy: how to handle the increasing number of clubs that had been paying their players in violation of NABBP rules on amateurism. But the writings of Albert Spalding hint that the issue of race remained very much on the minds of the white men in charge of the baseball establishment—and that the issues of race and professionalism were not entirely separate.

In retrospect, it is clear that from the moment baseball spread beyond the original four or five gentlemanly New York City clubs of the late 1840s and early 1850s, strict amateurism in baseball was doomed. While over the following two decades the NABBP continued to pay lip service to the amateur ideal, it took no real action to fight creeping professionalization among its member clubs. The truth is that the process could not have been reversed even if the NABBP had used all of its authority and prestige to try to do so. As far back as 1860, Brooklyn Excelsior pitcher Jim Creighton, the greatest star of his time, was rumored to have drawn a salary. In 1862 William Cammeyer saw a way to take advantage of the large crowds that came to watch such teams as the Atlantics and Mutuals. He built the nation's first enclosed ball field, the Union Grounds, in Williamsburg, Brooklyn. Admission was ten cents. Brooklyn clubs quite understandably demanded a share of the gate receipts. This soon led to teams playing for a larger, winner's share; in effect they were now playing for money. Strictly amateur teams like the tradition-bound Knickerbockers, who refused to play where admission was collected, found themselves part of a smaller and smaller minority. In 1866 a scandal erupted over allegations that four members of the Philadelphia Athletics, including Brooklynite Al

Reach, were being paid straight salaries by the club. The NABBP dropped the matter when the accused did not bother to show up at a hearing to answer the charges.

By the late 1860s the situation had come to a head. With a great many players on the better teams being paid under the table or through no-show jobs, cheating and double-dealing were rampant. One consequence of pretending that the players were not paid was that there was no standard contract or uniform labor-management agreement that regulated player movement. The result was an outbreak of "revolving," or contract jumping, as players traveled from team to team, even in midseason, to follow the highest bidder.

It is a telling commentary on the emptiness of the amateur ideal in 1868 that Henry Chadwick, the chairman of the NABBP rules committee and a man who was regarded as the conscience of baseball, attacked the revolvers for their disloyalty but did not even mention their violation of the amateur ethic. That same year, the NABBP institutionalized its own hypocrisy by setting up a classification system—similar to that of the modern NCAA—that divided NABBP members into an upper and a lower class. Everyone understood that the upper class, was in effect, the pros. This compromise failed to last one season. In 1869, Harry Wright assembled a virtual all-star team to play for his Cincinnati Red Stockings and announced that they would play as open professionals. Wright brought in Fred Waterman of the New York Mutuals, George Wright of the Unions of Morrisania (now part of the Bronx, New York City), Asa Brainard of the Brooklyn Excelsiors, Cal McVey of the Indianapolis Actives, and Charlie Sweasy and Andy Leonard of the Irvingtons of New Jersey. Only one player, first baseman Charlie "Bushel Basket"

Gould, was a native of Cincinnati. All were signed to one-year contracts at large salaries. Wright's powerhouse rolled over the competition, going 57–0 in 1869 and 22–0 in 1870 before finally losing to the Brooklyn Atlantics in extra innings. The Red Stockings' success inspired some of the better clubs to go professional and hopelessly alienated the others. The NABBP tried to heal the rift in its ranks by finding a compromise that would somehow both recognize the reality of open professionalism and placate the amateurs. In the end the NABBP failed to accomplish this and went out of existence, to be replaced in 1871 by the first modern professional league, the National Association of Professional Base Ball Players, or National Association, as it was known.

In his 1911 book Albert Spalding offers a revealing glimpse into the debate over professionalism that took place within baseball during the final days of the old NABBP, in 1869 and 1870. As Spalding tells it, there were three main factions. One was the gambling element, which favored the status quo. This is not surprising, since gamblers were able to take advantage of the weakness of the NABBP and the hypocritical atmosphere prevalent in baseball to bribe players, manipulate odds and scores, and even to fix the outcomes of games. Another element was the rank-and-file membership of the NABBP, which was content to tolerate some bending of the rules on amateurism but could not compete with the new breed of professional clubs such as the Red Stockings. These clubs correspond to the lower classification in the compromise of 1868. The last of the three elements is described by Spalding as:

> *that portion of the public—and it was at that time probably in the majority—who believed that baseball was simply an ordinary form of*

outdoor sport, a pastime, like cricket in
England, to be played in times of leisure, and
by gentlemen, for exercise, and only inciden-
tally for the entertainment of the public ... This
class felt that the game would suffer by pro-
fessionalism; that it meant the introduction
into the ranks of any man who could play the
game skillfully, without regard to his "race,
color or previous condition of servitude." It
meant, they thought, the introduction of row-
dies, drunkards and deadbeats.[5]

The reference to race, using the language of the
Fifteenth Amendment, seems surprisingly frank to
the modern reader. This is because there is no pre-
tense here that African Americans could not compete
with whites on the baseball field—the common excuse
for excluding African Americans from the major
leagues in the twentieth century. What Spalding is
saying is that a key reason for holding on to the amateur ethic in baseball in the 1860s was to justify and
preserve the color line. If baseball players played for
pay they would be judged solely on performance, not
on social standing. And if that were to happen, then
how could competent African Americans be kept out?

A BALLPLAYER FROM COOPERSTOWN

Post-Reconstruction America and the Strange Career of Bud Fowler

It took a few years, but Albert Spalding's "majority of the public"—who feared that the end of amateurism in baseball would lead to integration—turned out to be right. After the collapse of the old NABBP and the birth of baseball's first professional leagues, African-American ballplayers began here and there to cross the color line. The sport of baseball was not the only part of white society that opened up to some degree to African Americans. The ten years after the end of Reconstruction in 1877 was a time of tremendous liberalization and improvement in race relations in many corners of American life, both in the North and in the South. Still, fundamental racial problems remained. No matter how far integration progressed, acceptance of African Americans in baseball and other formerly all-white professions was mostly grudging and always tentative. African-American ballplayers enjoyed little job security. When a white team desperately needed his services, the African-American player was eagerly recruited, but when white talent became plentiful his welcome quickly wore out.

Even the small degree of integration that base-ball did achieve in this period would never have been possible without the professionalization of the game and the dizzying expansion that followed. The twenty years following the collapse of the NABBP saw the creation of dozens of new leagues with hundreds of new teams—and thousands of new playing jobs that had to be filled. It all started early in 1871, when the amateur clubs walked out of the NABBP convention, once and for all finishing that organization and baseball's amateur pretensions. On St. Patrick's Day of that same year, men from ten professional clubs met at Collier's bar on Broadway in New York City to form the openly professional National Association (NA). The predominantly northeastern group of clubs at that historic meeting included most of the baseball powers of the day: the Philadelphia Athletics, the Troy Haymakers, the Washington Olympics, the New York Mutuals, the Boston Red Stockings, the Rockford Forest Cities, the Cleveland Forest Cities, the Chicago White Stockings, the Fort Wayne Kekiongas, and the Brooklyn Eckfords. All started the 1871 National Association season except for the Eckfords, who did not decide to commit the ten dollars required for entry into the league until midseason.

The National Association was much better organized than the NABBP. It set clear criteria for the national championship, and it had a central office with some authority over clubs and players. But the NA was still very different from the professional leagues of today. Unlike modern professional teams, for example, its clubs could play "barnstorming," or exhibition, games against NA or non-NA clubs at any time before, during, or after the regular season; most NA clubs actually played most of their games and made most of their money outside the league structure.

The NA folded in 1875 after only five seasons of operation. There were two main reasons for the NA's collapse. One was corruption. Its central office did not have enough authority to keep out the gamblers who had helped to ruin the NABBP. It was also unable to resist being corrupted from within by its most powerful franchise, the Philadelphia Athletics. When star infielder and former batting champion Davy Force signed contracts with both Chicago and Philadelphia for the 1875 season, a bitter dispute broke out between the two clubs over who owned Force's services. The matter was referred to the NA central office. At first the NA ruled that Force must stay with Chicago, but then Philadelphia interests influenced the league to reverse the decision on flimsy grounds and send Force to the Athletics. This episode permanently damaged the NA's credibility.

The other reason for the death of the NA was Harry Wright's Boston Red Stockings. Powered by the nucleus of the original Cincinnati Red Stockings of 1869—McVey, Gould, George Wright, and Harry Wright himself—plus new stars Ross Barnes and Al Spalding, Boston was simply too good for the competition. Except for 1871, when Boston shortstop George Wright (Harry's brother and the league's best player) missed most of the season with an injury, the Red Stockings ran away with every NA pennant. From 1872 to 1875 they compiled unreal winning percentages of .830, .729, .743, and .899! Many clubs deteriorated under the pressure and failed to complete their schedules, and fan interest declined; twenty-five clubs came and went during the NA's brief existence. Even Red Stockings rooters stopped buying tickets; in at least one of its four championship seasons, Boston actually lost money.

The NA was replaced in 1876 by the National League (NL), just as the NABBP had been replaced by the NA. Like its two predecessors, the National League strictly observed the tradition of the baseball color line. With the possible exception of the case of Cuban native Esteban "Steve" Bellan—who played fifty-nine games for Troy and New York in the early 1870s before returning home to become an important pioneer in the development of Cuban baseball—the pattern established by the first baseball clubs held. Neither the NA nor the NL admitted a single African-American club or African-American player in the nineteenth century. As usual, there was no written rule excluding them, only a gentleman's agreement. Behind the scenes, however, the rationale for the color line was eroding quickly during this period. An artifact of the amateur baseball world, it would not survive the sweeping changes of the late 1870s and early 1880s.

The power behind the National League was Chicagoan William Hulbert, the former NA owner who had lost the Davy Force case. The new league had a stronger central authority and was much more firmly under the control of the owners than the NA had ever been. In previous baseball organizations, players had participated in the running of the game; one player, Robert Ferguson, even held the office of NA president. In Hulbert's new league, however, baseball was run as a business. Reflecting the values of the industrial revolution that was speedily transforming American life throughout the mid-nineteenth century, capitalists like Hulbert managed the sport themselves and reduced the players to mere employees. Baseball's new structure made sense to the business community, and the game began to attract a flood of new investors. America's newly built network of railroads stimulated the economies of the major cities in which most baseball fans lived and made it easier and cheaper for ball clubs to travel.

*The Cuban Giants were the first great
African-American professional club.*

In 1877 the first three minor leagues were formed.
Two of these organizations—the International
Association and the League Alliance—fell into an
arrangement with the National League that resembles today's major league–minor league structure.
While they were independent and had no formal relationship, they learned to respect each other's territo-
ries and player contracts. Although some so-called
minor-league clubs of the 1880s were as strong or
stronger than some National League clubs, a general
understanding developed that the National League
was the major league and the best players would play
their way up to the majors from the minors. As president of the National League, Hulbert invented the

reserve clause, a provision that gave management the right to renew a certain number of player contracts at will. The reserve clause made investing in baseball clubs safer by eliminating free agency and discouraging player movement. It allowed a club to keep its top players indefinitely—and without having to bid against other clubs for their services.

The business of baseball prospered under these new arrangements, and the next ten years saw an explosion in the formation of professional leagues and clubs. While many of these new clubs were short-lived, and while there was much bickering and conflict among leagues, clubs, and players, on the whole the 1880s was a decade of experimentation, expansion, and progress for professional baseball. At the major league level, after 1878 the National League stayed constant at eight teams, but a second major league—called the American Association—fielded six major league teams in 1882, eight in 1883, and thirteen in 1884. A third major league, the Union Association, fielded twelve major league teams in 1884. The minor leagues expanded even more dramatically. After the Tripartite Agreement formalized the major league–minor league relationship in 1883, creating the beginning of what we now call organized baseball, the number of important minor leagues mushroomed to seventeen by 1890. This does not include the dozens of smaller or less important minor leagues that came and went during this time.

Somewhere in the midst of these revolutionary changes in baseball, the color line began to unravel. Feeling few ties to the amateur traditions of the NABBP, a number of the new minor league clubs saw no reason not to sign promising African-American players. Many hired members away from some of the ace African-American independent teams that had been formed after the success of the famous Cuban

Giants, the first great African-American professional club. In spite of the team's name, none of the Cuban Giants was Cuban or Hispanic; the term *Cuban* was a common euphemism of the time for African-American. Expectations about integration in baseball reached the point that in 1887 one older African-American league—the Northern-based League of Colored Baseball Clubs—won admission to organized baseball as a minor league. The African-American league's purpose in joining organized baseball was to protect its roster from raiding by white minor league clubs. The *Sporting Life,* a national sports newspaper, in an editorial headed "Do They Need Protection?" scoffed at the suggestion that the new African-American league would have to worry about such raids.

> *The league can get along without protection . . . There is not likely to be much of a scramble for colored players. Only two such players are now employed on professional white clubs and the number is not likely to be ever materially increased owing to the high standard of play required and to the popular prejudice against any considerable mixture of the races.*[1]

The *Sporting Life* was wrong. By the end of the 1890s at least fifty-five African Americans would play on white teams in organized baseball. The story of the color line might have been very different if the League of Colored Baseball Clubs had survived and maintained its status as a minor league. It is difficult to imagine how or when organized baseball could have expelled an entire African-American league, considering how reluctant white baseball always has been to admit that the color line existed or to address issues of race in public. Unfortunately, the League of Colored

Baseball Clubs went out of business almost instantly. As African-American baseball player, executive, and historian Sol White wrote in 1907:

> *The League, on the whole, was without substantial backing and consequently did not last a week. But the short time of its existence served to bring out the fact that colored ball players of ability were numerous.*
>
> *The teams, with the exception of the Keystone, of Pittsburgh, and the Gorham, of New York, were composed mostly of home talent, so they were not necessarily compelled to disband. With reputations as clubs from the defunct Colored League, they proved to be very good drawing cards in different sections of the country. The Keystones and Gorhams, especially, distinguished themselves by later defeating the Cuban Giants.* [2]

Most African-American players of the 1880s remained with such all-African-American clubs as the Giants, Keystones, and Gorhams, but a few of the best players entered organized baseball and gradually worked their way up to the high minors. A pair of brothers, Fleet and Welday Walker, even reached the major leagues.

To understand how the baseball color line weakened in the 1880s, you have to step back and look at what was happening at that time in American race relations in general. Reconstruction had been brought to an end by a political deal, called the Compromise of 1877, that gave Rutherford B. Hayes the presidency. In exchange for the votes of Southern Democrats, Hayes agreed to withdraw federal troops from the South. One by one the Southern states threw off Reconstructionist rule in favor of locally controlled governments. Many people today consider this deal a Northern betrayal of the principles of Reconstruction that led directly to the denial of African-American voting and other civil rights and the rise of Jim Crow. However, while the Compromise of 1877 marked a falling off of Northern enthusiasm for racial reform, it did not mean an immediate end of all progress in race relations in the South.

The gains of twelve years of Reconstruction were not so easily turned back. The rise of Jim Crow in the South was slow and indirect. The first few years following the Compromise of 1877 were characterized by a consolidation of the progress made in race relations that had begun under Reconstruction. Racial attitudes had not yet hardened; they were in flux and varied widely from city to city and state to state. Radical racist views could be found on the editorial pages of some newspapers in upstate New York and Canada, while more moderate opinions could be found in newspapers in Charleston, South Carolina, and Richmond, Virginia. In most places, however, radical white supremacist ideas had no place in the political mainstream. Extreme racism was not considered respectable. For the most part, the ten years from 1877 to 1887 were a period of relative racial tolerance unparalleled in American history until very recent times.

Much to the surprise of many Northerners of the time, this was as true in the South as it was in the North. In his book *The Strange Career of Jim Crow,* historian C. Vann Woodward quotes from accounts by visitors to the post-Reconstruction South who were astounded to discover how well Reconstruction had worked. Expecting to see intimidation, hostility, or harsh treatment of African Americans, these Northern or European outsiders found instead "a condition of outward peace." There was no sign of Jim Crow laws or any other type of segregation lurking around the corner. The Ku Klux Klan lay dormant. Perhaps some of these visitors were surprised because of their ignorance of life in the prewar South. While slaves were obviously exploited and mistreated—slavery is by definition dehumanizing and inhumane—they were not segregated in the modern sense. On the contrary, slavery required that African Americans and slave-owning whites live and work close to each other. And as the great African American leader W. E. B. DuBois later pointed out, immediately after the war many ex-slaves worked as domestic servants, a situation that occasionally produced "bonds of intimacy, affection, and sometimes blood relationship between the races." In the post-Reconstruction days it was not at all unusual to see Southern whites and African Americans attending the same churches or sharing integrated public transportation.

Colonel Thomas W. Higginson, a prominent abolitionist who had led an African-American regiment in the U.S. Army during the Civil War (and who discovered the poet Emily Dickinson), traveled to the South in 1878 expecting to find the reforms of Reconstruction being dismantled. He wrote home instead that he saw no plan to endanger African-American rights on streetcars, at the polls, in courts, or in legislatures. "How," he wondered, "can we ask more of the states formerly in rebellion, than that they should be abreast of New England in granting rights and privileges to the colored race?" On his trip to the South in 1885, T. McCants Stewart, an African American who had left South Carolina for Boston ten years earlier, made an observation that has been made countless times since: "I think," he said, "that whites of the South are really less afraid to have contact with colored people than the whites of the North."[3]

Up to a point, whites and African Americans in the post-Reconstruction South shared the national pastime as well. There was an African-American base-ball tradition in the South going back to the Civil War. In some places it went back much further than that. A 1797 law on the books of Fayetteville, North Carolina, for instance, specifically prohibited African Americans from playing baseball on Sundays. And in the days of slavery before the Civil War, communities of free African Americans had existed in many Southern towns. Some of these contained a middle class that supported baseball clubs, just as the African-American middle class in Philadelphia supported the Pythians. Throughout the 1880s African-American amateur clubs sprang up all over the South, particularly around New Orleans and on the Gulf Coast. Because of the more relaxed local Spanish and French racial traditions, African-American clubs from these areas had relationships with white clubs, some as close as had existed in Philadelphia, Washington, D.C., and Brooklyn during the 1850s and 1860s. Just as in the North, there were informal interracial contests. In many places white and African-American fans mixed freely in a way that would be completely unthinkable in the Jim Crow days that were to come.

These African-American clubs in the Deep South underwent the same movement toward professionalism as white clubs. When African Americans organized the first African-American professional league, they met not in Philadelphia, Washington, or Brooklyn, but in Jacksonville, Florida.

This first African-American baseball league, called the Southern League of Colored Baseballists (SLCB), opened for business in the Spring of 1886. It included ten member clubs from Memphis, Atlanta, Savannah, Charleston, Jacksonville, and New Orleans. Like its Northern successor, the League of Colored Baseball Clubs, the SLCB folded within a year because of money problems. While it lasted, however, it was reported on by the white as well as by the African-American press and was well attended by baseball fans of both races. According to the opening day coverage in the *New Orleans Picayune,* "Judging from the first game the colored clubs will furnish good sport and the teams can play ball. The [Memphis] Eclipse boys all fielded well and threw the ball like the best professionals."

BUD FOWLER

As far as integration and racial tolerance went in the South of the late 1870s and 1880s, it never reached the point of whites and African Americans playing on the same professional baseball team. The first African American to enter organized baseball was a Northerner. His name is John Fowler. He was known as "Bud" because of his habit of calling strangers by that name.

Bud Fowler was born John W. Jackson in 1858 in a rural area near, of all places, Cooperstown, New York. His father moved the family into town the following year and set up shop as a barber. Neither the Jacksons nor anyone else in America had any idea that in the twentieth century Cooperstown would be selected as the site of Abner Doubleday's mythical first baseball game or that millions of people would travel there to visit the National Baseball Hall of Fame and Museum. It is an interesting irony that the Hall of Fame, which commemorates the history of a sport whose Jim Crow policies excluded African Americans and dark-skinned Hispanics for most of its 122 years of existence, shares a birthplace with Fowler, the first and possibly greatest African-American ballplayer of the nineteenth century.

After serving an apprenticeship with a well-known Washington, D.C., African-American amateur club,

Bud Fowler, one of the greatest African-American players of the nineteenth century, is shown in 1885 in a team picture of the Keokuk club of Iowa in the Western League.

the Mutuals, in 1872 Fowler played on his first white team, in New Castle, Pennsylvania. His career in white baseball ended in 1895, when he was thirty-seven years old, with Adrian of the Michigan State League. In between he played with twenty teams in thirteen leagues, never staying more than one season with the same team and never making it out of the minor leagues. The reason for all this movement was not any lack of ability or character. Fowler was a solid citizen and an outstanding athlete. In a few cases the reason was that his team—like so many in that turbulent time—moved, went broke, or disbanded. In other cases the reason was racial prejudice.

Over the course of his two decades in white professional baseball, Bud Fowler's career typified the experience of dozens of other African Americans who would cross the color line after him. For one thing, Fowler never knew what to expect from white fans, teammates, or the press. In most communities in which he played, Fowler was the first African-American player anyone had ever seen playing on a white club. Reaction to him ranged from respect or even affection to irrational hatred and everything in between. The newspapers that covered Fowler are full of weird remarks about the color of his skin that show how ill at ease many white fans and reporters were with the idea of integrated baseball. A newspaper in Denver, for example, included in its scouting report on Fowler the observation that he was safe from sunburn and "don't tan a cent." The *Sporting Life,* mocking clubs that tried to pass off African-American players as "Spaniards" or "Indians," wrote that "some say that Fowler is a colored man, but we account for his dark complexion by the fact that ... in chasing balls [he] has become tanned from constant and careless exposure to the sun."

When his skin color became too troublesome an issue for the club that employed him, Fowler would be cut loose. He would then return to his off-season job, barbering, or put on exhibitions of long-distance walking and running. According to one newspaper he ran a mile in under five minutes, an excellent time in those days. In between races and barbering jobs, he would search for another baseball job in yet another city.

Like most of his African-American successors in white baseball, Fowler found that he had to be much better than a white player even to be considered for a job. As a rule African Americans who played on nineteenth-century white teams—especially in the high minor leagues—were stars; baseball had a definite policy of "no mediocre African Americans need apply." Finally, as determined as Fowler was to overcome the difficult conditions he found in the organized minor leagues, in the end he was worn down and driven back into the world of African-American baseball. Speaking to a reporter shortly after his retirement, Fowler evaluated his career. "My skin is against me," he said, "If I had been not quite so black, I might have caught on as a Spaniard or something of that kind. The race prejudice is so strong that my black skin barred me."[4] Many contemporary white sportswriters agreed. In 1885 a reporter from the *Sporting Life* rated Fowler as "one of the best general players in the country." "If he had a white face," the story continued, "he would be playing with the best of them." Another white newspaper called him "one of the best pitchers on the continent of America." Reading descriptions of his brilliant and sometimes flamboyant play in the minors—the poet Carl Sandburg recalled that as a boy he had once seen Fowler show off by playing an entire game at second base *left-handed*—there is a sense that he was often playing at least a level or two below his ability. Without a doubt, if Fowler had been white his talent would have taken him to the major league ball parks of big cities like New York, Chicago, and St. Louis instead of the dusty diamonds of Keokuk, Topeka, and Santa Fe.

Fowler's first appearance in a white professional league was in 1878 with Lynn of the International Association, the first minor league, which was in its first year of existence. Lynn picked him up after seeing him pitch the Chelsea, Massachusetts, town team to a 2–1 victory over the defending NL champions, the Boston Red Stockings. Fowler's opponent in that game was ace pitcher Tommy Bond, who had led the NL the previous season with 40 wins, a winning percentage of .702, and an ERA of 2.11. After brief stays with Lynn, and with Worcester of the New England League, Fowler spent the next six years playing for various American and Canadian clubs and working as a barber between stops. In Canada, the Guelph Maple Leafs released him because of his race. The local newspaper scolded the Maple Leafs for being "ill-natured enough to object to the colored pitcher Fowler . . . he has forgotten more baseball than the present team ever knew."

Fowler returned to organized baseball in 1884 with the Stillwater, Minnesota, team of the competitive Northwestern League. There he batted .302 and won seven games as a pitcher for a very poor team that won only twenty-two for the season. He became a fan favorite, the *Stillwater Sun* calling him a "colored bonanza." After Stillwater folded, Fowler signed with Keokuk of the Western League as a second baseman. There is some question about whether Fowler's move from the pitcher's mound to second base was caused by an arm injury or by the fact that hostile teammates would sometimes intentionally play poorly behind him. Being sabotaged by their own fielders was an unfortunate fact of life for many nineteenth-century African-American pitchers on white teams. Either way, the position change gave Fowler no trouble; that year the *Sporting Life* said that "those who know say that there is no better second baseman in the country; [Fowler] is both a good batter and a fine base runner."

In 1886 he moved on again to Topeka, also of the Western League, where he hit .309 and led the league in triples.

It was in Binghamton, New York, in the International League (IL), the best league that Fowler played in, that he encountered the worst racial hostility of his career. Fowler was not the only African-American player in the IL at this time; Frank Grant played for Buffalo, and Fleet Walker and George Stovey played for Newark. But there was a lot of opposition around the league to the hiring of African Americans. One IL veteran anonymously told the *Sporting Life* in 1889:

> *I could not help pitying some of the poor black fellows that played in the International League. Fowler used to play second base with the lower part of his legs encased in wooden guards. He knew that about every player that came down to second base on a steal had it in for him and would, if possible, throw the spikes into him. He was a good player, but left the base every time there was a close play in order to get away from the spikes.*[5]

Fowler hit .350 for Binghamton but was released in mid-July after the IL board of directors discouraged member clubs from signing African Americans. Binghamton paid Fowler the ironic compliment of including in his release the provision that he could not sign with any of Binghamton's competitors. After 1887, baseball jobs began to dry up for African Americans, especially in the Northeast. Bud Fowler found it harder and harder to find work in organized baseball—until, after the 1895 season, he gave up.

A talented, energetic man, Bud Fowler devoted much of the rest of his life to developing African-American baseball. Praised by Sol White as "the celebrated promoter of colored baseball clubs and the sage of baseball," Fowler joined the Cuban Giants, the first great African-American professional club. He also founded a number of famous barnstorming clubs, including the Page Fence Giants and the All-

American Black Tourists. In 1904 he failed in an attempt to organize a new African-American league called the National Colored Baseball League. He died at his sister's home in Frankfort in upstate New York at fifty-five years of age and was buried in an unmarked grave about twenty-five miles from Cooperstown.

FALSE SPRING

Fleet Walker and the Grudging Integration of the 1880s

The next African Americans to cross the baseball color line after Bud Fowler in 1878 were first baseman Jack Frye with Reading, Pennsylvania, of the Interstate Association and catcher Fleet Walker with Toledo, Ohio, of the Northwestern League, both in 1883. In the four years after that, the trickle of African-American players into organized baseball increased to a small but steady flow; there were three African-American players on white teams in 1884, three in 1885, five in 1886, and ten in 1887.

This integration of baseball was, with two exceptions, limited to the minors. And it followed a definite pattern: an African-American player might be allowed to cross the color line if there were an extreme need for that player's particular skills; if the black player was a star; if the white team was in a minor league; and if the white team played in states in the Northeast, upper Midwest, or West.

Even when all these conditions were met and an African-American player was able to cross the color line, however, he was accepted for as short a time as absolutely necessary. At the first sign of protest or other trouble, he would be quickly released to return to the world of the African-American independent teams such as the Cuban Giants. Most African-American players, therefore, who played on white teams in this period made several trips back and forth across the color line.

The major leagues were more resistant than the minor leagues to the idea of hiring African Americans. One reason for this is that African-American talent was less in demand because there were fewer jobs in the majors. Another is that the major leagues of the 1880s considered themselves the guardians of baseball tradition. They were much more influenced by the old Northeastern ideal of respectability that was the legacy of the lily-white NABBP than were the minor leagues.

Of the fifty-five or so African Americans known to have played in organized baseball in the nineteenth century, only two—Fleet Walker and his brother Welday—played in the majors. They did so for only one year, 1884, and then for only forty-two games and five games, respectively. The brothers reached the majors partly by chance when their team, Toledo, Ohio, of the Northwestern League, transferred to the American Association for the 1884 season. The American Association (AA), which lasted from 1882 to 1891, played alongside the NL as a second major league. Starting in 1884, the champions of both leagues played an annual postseason series that was similar to today's World Series between the NL and the American League.

There was, at least in the pretensions of the NL, a definite class difference between the NL and its younger rival, the AA. The NL's stronger commitment to the color line in baseball was part of that class difference. It was no accident that it was the newer AA and not the older, more conservative NL that accepted the Walker brothers even for part of one season.

NL founder William Hulbert had made it clear from the beginning that his league intended to set a high moral standard. In language that echoes the charters of the old New York amateur clubs of the 1840s and 1850s, the original NL constitution of 1876 states, "The object of this organization is to encourage, foster and elevate the game of baseball . . . and to make baseball playing respectable and honorable." Hulbert soon removed any doubt about whether the NL would back up these words; in 1877 he banned four members of the Louisville club for life for conspiring with gamblers to throw games. The NL also demonstrated a typically middle-class distaste for excessive drinking among its players. Year after year the annual official baseball guides of the 1870s and 1880s railed against the mixture of alcohol and professional baseball. Speaking to NL players in 1876, a baseball guide called the "Beadle's Dime Centennial Baseball Player," preached,

Any man now desirous of using his physical and mental powers to their utmost advantage, must ignore first, intemperance in eating and second, refuse to allow a drop of alcoholic liquor, whether in the form of spirits, wine or beer, to pass down his throat.[1]

In 1881 Hulbert established a blacklist for players who were considered undesirable because of drinking, crookedness, excessive debt, or unsportsmanlike conduct on the playing field. No player whose name appeared on this list could be hired by an NL team.

The National League excluded working-class fans as "undesirable" as well. NL clubs charged a steep fifty cents—in a time when a first-class hotel room cost about two dollars—for admission to their games and scheduled weekday games for the middle to late afternoon. Game time was usually forty-five minutes or so after the end of the typical white-collar worker's office hours. They allowed no games on Sunday and prohibited the sale of beer or any alcoholic beverage in their ballparks. Considering that the working-class workweek stretched to ten or even twelve hours a day, Monday through Saturday, these measures essentially restricted major league baseball to the middle and upper economic classes.

When the American Association was formed in 1882, part of its marketing strategy was to appeal to the forgotten working-class fan. The AA charged only twenty-five cents for admission, held games on Sunday wherever local laws permitted, and sold beer and whiskey at its parks. It was this—the working man's major league—that for one brief moment allowed one of its teams to field a pair of African-American players. The stuffier NL, on the other hand, stuck to the gentleman's agreement excluding African Americans. In doing so, the NL saw itself as the last bastion of a long-standing baseball tradition—a tradition that was ready, within a very few years, to make a comeback.

In the meantime, however, integration in the minors reached its peak in the middle to late 1880s. By 1887 there had been more than a dozen different African-American players on white teams, although the number who saw significant playing time is smaller than that. The following are the seven players who played four or more seasons in organized baseball in the nineteenth century:

- Bud Fowler—eight seasons
- Fleet Walker—seven seasons
- George Stovey—six seasons

- Frank Grant—six seasons
- Sol White—five seasons
- Jack Frye—five seasons
- Richard Johnson—four seasons.[2]

The biggest stars of this group are the five players at the top of the list: Fowler, Walker, Stovey, Grant, and White. These men were more than just outstanding athletes; they were extraordinary in every way. Considering all the obstacles that baseball and white society in general put in their way, they had to be. By their courage, determination, and sheer skill, these five players made themselves indispensable to white teams that, in many cases, would have been happy to have had a good excuse for releasing them. With every base hit, stolen base, or strikeout, these five kept up the pressure on baseball's weakened color line. As long as they and other African-American ballplayers continued to take the field and help their teams win, no one in organized baseball could pretend that the color line was anything but plain, simple bigotry.

FLEET WALKER

Moses Fleetwood "Fleet" Walker was unusually well educated for a professional ballplayer of the 1880s, a decade when total illiterates in baseball probably outnumbered players with college degrees. The son of a minister from Steubenville, Ohio, Walker attended Oberlin College, a school with a tradition of civil rights activism, from 1877 to 1881. He was not there to play baseball. Walker followed a liberal arts curriculum that included science, math, Latin, Greek, German, engineering, zoology, and rhetoric. Only in his final year did Oberlin field a baseball team. In 1882 Walker transferred to the University of Michigan, where he

The Oberlin College, Ohio, baseball team of 1881. Fleet Walker is number six and his brother Welday is number ten.

started at the position of catcher on the varsity baseball team for two years. Photographs from his college days show a tall, handsome man with a serious expression; people who knew him remembered him as intelligent and gentlemanly. In short, Fleet Walker was just the kind of respectable, middle-class athlete who, had he been white, would have been considered a credit to the National League.

Walker may have been a gentleman, but he was also strong and tough. In those days most catchers played without gloves and wore little protective gear above the shins. Considering how often catchers of the 1880s took the field with swollen, split fingers; broken noses; and sore rib cages, it is a wonder that any of them managed to play more than half of their team's games. It is certainly no surprise that many of them batted under .200 for a season.

Walker went professional in 1883 and joined Toledo, Ohio, of the Northwestern League. Again starting at catcher, he helped Toledo win the pennant with steady defense and a .251 batting average in sixty games. The following year the Toledo franchise joined the American Association and brought along its top players. Fleet Walker was one of them.

Walker was tremendously popular among the fans of Toledo, but reaction to him in the rest of the league was, as usual, mixed. There was no denying his ability. He started over Deacon McGuire, a lefty-throwing catcher who would go on to play twenty-six seasons in the majors, and batted .263 over forty-two games. Walker's batting average was excellent in the context of the 1884 AA; the whole league batted only .240 that year. And he surely would have played in many more games if a foul tip hadn't broken one of his ribs and knocked him out of action in July.

Walker's season did not end soon enough for fans in some AA cities. In Louisville, racist fans booed and heckled him, provoking a Toledo newspaper to comment:

> [Walker's] poor playing in a city where the Color Line is closely drawn as it is in Louisville . . . should not be counted against him. Many a good player under less aggravating circumstances than this, has become rattled and unable to play. It is not creditable to the Louisville management that it should permit such outrageous behavior to occur on its grounds.[3]

In more tolerant AA cities, the combination of Walker and Irish-born pitcher Tony "The Count" Mullane was a surefire gate attraction. Aside from the ethnic novelty of the Walker-Mullane battery, they were an effective combination on the field. Even though Toledo finished 12 games under .500 and 27½ games out of first place, Mullane had one of his finest seasons with Fleet Walker catching him. He pitched in 68 games, completed 65, and won 37—statistics second only to those of league leader Guy Hecker—and he led the AA in shutouts, with 8. Remembering the 1884 season years later, Mullane called Walker "the best catcher I ever worked with." But Fleet Walker's 1884 defensive performance may have been even better than it appears from the statistics. Mullane went on to say in the same interview that "I disliked a Negro and whenever I pitched to him I used to pitch anything I wanted without looking at his signals."[4]

In October of 1884, Walker and Toledo became involved in an unpleasant racial incident in Richmond, Virginia, that goes a long way toward explaining why no African-American player from this time ever played with a white team in the South. Several weeks before the team's scheduled series at Richmond, the Toledo manager received a threatening letter that resembles those sent to the Brooklyn Dodgers during Jackie Robinson's rookie season sixty-three years later:

> *We the undersigned do hereby warn you not to put up Walker, the Negro catcher, the evenings that you play in Richmond, as we could mention the names of 75 determined men who have sworn to mob Walker if he comes on the ground in a suit. We hope you will listen to our words of warning, so that there will be no trouble; but if you do not there certainly will be. We*

only write this to prevent much bloodshed, as
you alone can prevent.[5]

Whoever wrote this—the letter was signed with phony names—must not have been reading the sports pages very closely. Fleet Walker had already been seriously injured and he was released by Toledo for that reason weeks before the Richmond trip.

In 1885 a recovered Walker signed with Cleveland of the minor Western League, where he joined his brother Welday, who had filled in for a few games in the outfield with Toledo in 1884. Neither ever returned to the major leagues. Fleet Walker played in organized baseball through 1889, catching for Waterbury, Connecticut, in the Eastern League; Newark, New Jersey, in the International League; and finally Syracuse, New York, also in the International League. At Newark Walker was part of another ethnic curiosity. He and George Stovey formed the first-ever all–African-American battery in organized baseball. And like Walker and Mullane, they were promoted as a special gate attraction. "Verily they are dark horses," wrote the *Sporting Life* in 1887, "and ought to be a drawing card. No rainchecks given when they play." Walker retired at thirty-three on a high note after helping Syracuse to the 1889 IL pennant.

Like Bud Fowler, Fleet Walker was a multitalented man who without the color line might have contributed much more to baseball, both during and after his career. In both cases the loss was certainly baseball's. After leaving the game Walker returned to Steubenville, Ohio, where he became a successful businessman and a respected leader in the African-American community. He published a newspaper and in 1908 wrote *Our Home Colony,* a book arguing for African-American emigration to Africa. He was also an early entrepreneur in the movie business; he owned a movie theater and applied for a number of patents for inventions relating to movie technology.

GEORGE STOVEY

Pennsylvania-born left-handed pitcher George Stovey did not leave behind much in the way of statistics. No one kept accurate records of the Cuban Giants, the New York Gorhams, the Cuban X-Giants, and the other African-American independent teams, on which Stovey played for most of his career.

Stovey's brief time in organized baseball, however, was enough to prove that he was one of the finest African-American players of the decade and one of the finest pitchers, period. Playing for Jersey City in the Eastern League in 1886, he quickly acquired a reputation as a fiery competitor and a top pitcher. It is hard to say which was hotter, Stovey's blazing fastball or his temper. Jersey City manager and future IL president Pat Powers called him "one of the greatest pitchers in the country" but also "head-strong and obstinate, and, consequently, hard to manage." Newspaper accounts tell of games in which Stovey would lose control of himself on the mound, putting on angry displays over bad fielding plays behind him or calls by umpires that went against him. In one 1891 Cuban Giants game, Stovey became enraged over an umpire's call at home plate and threw a live ball (one still in play) over the outfield fence, allowing three more runs to score.

In 1887 Stovey moved up to the Newark team in the International League. Newark planned to pair him with Fleet Walker in hopes that the veteran Walker would be a steadying influence on Stovey's emotions. It worked: Stovey won 34 games—a record in the International League, which has survived to this day—and lost only 14 with a 2.42 ERA. The league's best starting pitcher, he also filled in the outfield and batted .255 with 16 stolen bases in 208 at bats. With the exception of brief stops with Worcester, Massachusetts, and Troy, New York, in the low minors, after the IL drew the color line in 1887 Stovey played virtually the rest of his career with African-American teams.

FRANK GRANT

Many people consider second baseman Frank Grant, not Bud Fowler, the greatest African-American baseball player of the nineteenth century. One of their arguments is that Grant broke out of the cycle of transience that Fowler, Walker, and nearly every other African American fell into in organized baseball. Instead of moving constantly from one team to another, he was the only African American of his time to play three consecutive seasons with the same white club, Buffalo in the International League. As further testimony to his importance on the Buffalo team, after the IL's reinstitution of the color line in late 1887, Grant lasted through the 1888 season with Buffalo. He was one of the very last African Americans to be pushed out of the IL.

Born in Pittsfield, Massachusetts, in the middle 1860s, Grant joined Buffalo in 1886 after starting the season with Meriden, Connecticut, of the Eastern League. He became an instant star, hitting .344 in 1886, .353 in 1887, and .346 in 1888. In fact he batted .313 or higher in every one of his six seasons in organized baseball. Although below average in size, Grant could do it all in the field or at the plate. He hit for power, leading the IL in home runs and total bases, and was an excellent base runner. He regularly had stolen base totals in double digits and was famous

An 1887 photograph of the International League Buffalo Bisons. Frank Grant is second from right in front row.

for his ability to steal home. According to Sol White, Grant's play was "a revelation to his fellow teammates, as well as to the spectators. In hitting he ranked with the best and his fielding bordered on the impossible." He was frequently compared to the greatest white athletes; reporters nicknamed him the "Black Dunlap," after the NL's Fred Dunlap. Dunlap was a slick-fielding second baseman who once hit .412 in the Union Association, a third major league that operated in 1884. Grant was probably a better player than Dunlap. One of the greatest tributes from the white press to any nineteenth-century African-

American player came when the *Sporting Life* called Frank Grant the greatest all-around player ever to have played in Buffalo. Preceding Grant in Buffalo baseball were no less than four future Hall of Famers—Pud Galvin, Dan Brouthers, Orator O'Rourke, and Hoss Radbourne—as well as a number of other big-league stars.

As far as the fans of Buffalo were concerned, Grant was unquestionably the biggest star on the team. However, as with Walker and Fowler before him, Grant was not so popular among his fellow players and the fans in other cities. In a rare mention of African-American fans by the white press, one Boston newspaper noted Grant's popularity in Boston and added that he drew a large crowd of "gentlemen of his color, and not a few dusky dames," to the Boston ballpark. After Buffalo played a preseason exhibition series in Pittsburgh, a local newspaper called Grant "a sensation." But Grant's competitors were not always so appreciative. In a strange comment, the Pittsburgh manager criticized Grant's great fielding range. "No attention," he complained, "is paid to such a thing as running all over another man's territory." Grant was subjected to more than just disapproval. According to one white IL veteran, "about half the pitchers [tried] their best to hit these colored players when at the bat ... One of the International League pitchers pitched for Grant's head all the time. He never put a ball over the plate but sent them in straight and true right at Grant." In 1886 and 1888, his own teammates refused to pose with him for the team picture. They made it clear to Grant that the reason was nothing personal—just the color of his skin.

In the 1890s, after leaving organized baseball, Frank Grant played with the African-American teams the Cuban Giants and the New York Gorhams. In the early 1900s, Grant played with the Philadelphia

Giants, a prestigious African-American powerhouse that was organized by Walter Schlichter and managed by Sol White. Schlichter was the sports editor of the *Philadelphia City Item*, the same newspaper that had sponsored an interracial baseball match with the Pythians back in 1869. Grant retired in 1903, working for the rest of his life as a waiter in New York City.

He died in obscurity in 1937.

SOL WHITE

Solomon "Sol" White was born in Bellaire, Ohio, in 1868 and arrived in organized baseball a few years too late to have the impact of a Fowler or a Grant. Eighteen eighty-seven, the peak year of African-American representation in organized baseball, was his first year as a professional. He first joined the Pittsburgh Keystones of the short-lived League of Colored Baseball Clubs and later that season moved into white baseball with the Wheeling, West Virginia, team of the Ohio League.

White's first experience in white baseball was a pleasant one in many ways. Playing third base, he batted .370 and scored 54 runs in only 52 games and became a crowd favorite. When the Ohio League decided to follow the IL's lead and draw the color line for the 1888 season, however, White was out of a job. While the league claimed that its fans wanted the color line, this does not seem to have been true in Wheeling. When Grant returned there the next year with an African-American independent team, he received flowers and a standing ovation from the Wheeling fans.

White stayed on the African-American side of the color line for much of the rest of his career, although he made the most of his scattered and brief appearances with white teams. He batted .333 in 31 games with Trenton, New Jersey, in 1889, .356 in 54 games with York, Pennsylvania, in 1890; .375 in 4 games with Ansonia, Connecticut, in 1891; and .385 in 10 games with Fort Wayne, Indiana, in 1895.

White was well-traveled in African-American baseball, too. Throughout the 1890s he jumped from team to team and back again. At that time, African-American clubs were not organized into leagues; they issued and accepted challenges from their rivals as they wished, in much the same way white amateur clubs had operated in the 1850s and 1860s. At the end of most seasons, the two teams judged the best would meet to determine a consensus national champion.

A pattern developed in the 1890s: each year whichever team happened to have White would win the African-American championship. The following year the runner-up would hire away White and win the championship. In 1889 the New York Gorhams, with White on the team, beat the Cuban Giants to win the championship. White started the 1891 season with the Cubans but was rehired by the Gorhams. This Gorham team was the finest team in nineteenth-century African-American baseball and possibly one of the finest anywhere. With White playing second base, forming a double-play combination with Frank Grant at shortstop, and George Stovey pitching, the 1891 Gorhams played more than one hundred games and lost only four. In 1896 White helped Bud Fowler's Page Fence Giants to the championship over the Cuban X-Giants, and in 1897 he helped the Cuban X-Giants to that year's championship.

In 1902, a few years after the color line had been drawn in every major and minor league, *Philadelphia City Item* sports editor Walter Schlichter hired White as player-manager of a new African-American club sponsored by the newspaper and called the Philadelphia

The Philadelphia Giants dominated African American baseball in the first decade of the twentieth century. In the center, sitting in the chair, is newspaper editor Walter Schlichter, the team's owner. Player-manager Sol White is third from right in the back row. On Schlichter's left is Rube Foster and on Schlichter's right is Charlie Grant.

Giants. White built the team into a dynasty. He brought in the best available players, men such as Grant "Home Run" Johnson, Frank Grant, Charlie Grant, Andrew "Rube" Foster, Bruce Petway, and John Henry "Pop" Lloyd. The Philadelphia Giants dominated African-American baseball for a decade.

They did not win every national championship, but every year from 1902 through 1909 they were in the running.

White's Philadelphia Giants were champions in 1902 and were narrowly defeated by the Cuban X-Giants in 1903, thanks to a virtuoso pitching performance by Rube Foster. Foster was a terrific control pitcher who got his nickname from having beaten Philadelphia Athletics ace Rube Waddell in an exhibition game. Honus Wagner called Foster "the greatest pitcher I've ever seen."

White hired Foster away from the Cuban X-Giants in 1904, and the Philadelphia Giants and Cuban X-Giants met before a large crowd in Atlantic City, New Jersey, in a rematch for the 1904 championship. "Never in the annals of colored baseball," White would later write, "did two nines fight for supremacy as these teams fought." This time the series was closer, but once again Foster's pitching was the deciding factor. Philadelphia won, two games to one.

First as a player, then as a manager, promoter, and executive, White built a brilliant career spanning four decades. Winning seemed to follow him; wherever he went in baseball he was always around the best players, teams, and organizations.

White's greatest successes as a manager were the Philadelphia Giants teams of 1905 and 1906. The 1905 Giants went 134–21 and could not find a willing opponent for the African-American championship series, and the team of 1906 won 108 and lost only 31. When Rube Foster organized the first lasting Negro League in the 1920s, White served in various capacities, ranging from coaching to managing to the front office.

Even when he was working hard to develop African-American players, teams, and leagues, Sol White looked forward to the return of integration in organized baseball. He believed that the purpose of African-American professional baseball was to develop talent, build skills, and instill pride and professionalism in African-American players in order to prepare for the day when the color line would be broken completely and forever. This was one reason why White took every opportunity in the 1890s and 1900s to match his great African-American teams against top white clubs in exhibition games.

In 1902 the Philadelphia Giants challenged the American League pennant-winning Philadelphia Athletics; the Giants lost, but respectably, 8–3 and 13–9. White himself got three hits off big-league pitching in the second game. In 1904 they swept four games from the strong Newark Bears of the International League and were undefeated in a number of games against clubs from other minor leagues. White challenged organized baseball to pit the 1906 World Series winner against his Philadelphia Giants in order to "decide who can play baseball best, the white or black Americans." Perhaps remembering 1904, the white clubs gave no answer.

White's greatest off-field contribution to baseball may have been his 1907 book *Sol. White's Official Base Ball Guide*, which tells the story of African-American baseball from the early days to the turn of the century. The 1900s was a pivotal decade for African Americans. Men of White's generation were living through the heyday of Jim Crow in American history, yet they could remember a much more tolerant time. As White writes:

> *The colored ballplayer suffers great inconvenience at times while traveling. All hotels are generally filled from cellar to garret when they*

strike a town. It is a common occurrence for them to arrive in a city late and walk around for several hours before getting a place to lodge.

The situation is far different today in this respect than it was years ago. At one time the colored teams were accommodated in some of the best hotels in the country, as the entertainment in 1877* of the Cuban Giants at the McClure House in Wheeling, West Virginia will show.

The cause of this change is no doubt due to the condition of things from a racial standpoint. With the color question uppermost in the minds of the people at the present time, such proceedings on the part of hotel-keepers may be expected and will be difficult to remedy.[6]

White's book also provides box scores and photographs of contemporary African-American stars, and an essay on pitching from Rube Foster. Foster gives the following advice to young pitchers on how to handle a big inning: "Do not worry. Try to appear jolly and unconcerned. I have smiled often with the bases full and two strikes and three balls on the batter."

White also tells of his vision for baseball's future. "Some day," he writes, "the bar will drop and some good man will be chosen from out of the colored profession that will be a credit to all, and pave the way for others to follow." Sol White lived to see both this prophecy and his plan for African-American professional baseball fulfilled by Jackie Robinson and the dozens of Negro Leaguers who followed him into organized baseball in the 1940s and 1950s. Seventy-nine years old and living only a short subway ride from Ebbets Field, White was able to watch Jackie

*A misprint: actually it was 1887.

Robinson play for the Dodgers in 1947 in person. He lived until 1955, long enough to see that the second integration of baseball would be the last.

Fowler, Walker, Grant, Stovey, and White were able to cross the color line and play in white baseball for two main reasons. One was a temporary thaw in American race relations. The other was simple economic necessity—African-American players were needed to fill the greatly increasing number of professional baseball jobs in the 1880s. The number of African-American jobs in organized baseball expanded with the economy. It contracted with the economy, too. When America suffered a depression in 1891 and 1892, followed by a long period of sluggish economic growth, two things occurred: the number of baseball leagues and teams shrunk drastically, and the number of African Americans in white baseball dropped to zero. Either way, the accomplishments of Fowler and the others had been unthinkable before 1877 and would become unthinkable again soon after 1887.

How did white Americans of that time feel about this brief, partial integration of baseball? It is hard to say, because in those days there was little public discussion of race. The subject was taboo for white, middle-class society. Hardly any memoir or history book from this period mentions African Americans, even when discussing the middle 1880s—a time when baseball was dealing with important racial issues. Jacob Morse's 1888 book *Sphere and Ash,* for example, contains sixty-two pages on the history of baseball from its beginnings to contemporary times; there is not one word about African-American clubs, interracial exhibition games, Fleet Walker, or the color line. Baseball books by NL stars Cap Anson and John Montgomery Ward—two players who were squarely in the middle of the racial controversies of the 1880s—

are completely silent on the topic of baseball and the color line.

Since racial feelings are often expressed without words, photographs and pictures can offer clues to racial attitudes. Photographs of many integrated teams from the 1880s and 1890s show white players standing apart from or even physically shrinking from a solitary African-American player. The team photographs of the 1886 and 1888 Buffalo IL clubs tell us a lot by not telling us anything. The photos do not exist because the white players refused to pose with Frank Grant.

Just as the NABBP and NA had almost never discussed race on the record or put their racial policies into writing, the leagues of the 1880s and 1890s, with few exceptions, drew the color line and weeded out African-American players without holding a debate, passing a resolution, or making a public statement. Race was taboo in the press, too. Many newspapers of this time could not bring themselves to use words like "black" or "Negro" that directly refer to skin color. When they could not avoid writing about African Americans, they used euphemisms like "Cubans," "Spaniards," or "Ethiopians."

Obviously, for every African-American player who crossed the color line in the 1880s and 1890s, there were hundreds who played out their entire careers in African-American baseball. Little survives to tell us how these men felt about being excluded by the color line. How did the experience of crossing the color line affect the African-American players who did play in organized baseball? For Stovey and Grant it is difficult to say, but it is also hard to imagine that they were not bitter about their treatment; both must have known that they had enough talent to compete in the major leagues. Sol White used his baseball experiences in the most constructive way possible, but he spent less time in white baseball than the others. His lifetime of achievement may owe more to his energetic, optimistic personality than to any positive experience with integration.

For Fowler and Walker, the two players with the most longevity on white teams, the experience was a very bitter one. Nothing shows this better than their post-playing careers. When his playing days were over, Fowler created the All-American Black Tourists, the first of the clowning type of African-American barnstorming teams. The Tourists were very popular among white fans and inspired many imitators in the 1910s and 1920s. On the day of a game—which would usually be against a white team—the Tourists would make a showy entrance, strutting into town wearing top hats, sporting formal black evening dress, and twirling umbrellas. Upon request, they would play the game in these clothes instead of baseball uniforms.

Fleet Walker went to college with whites and in his twenties and thirties struggled hard to make it in the world of white baseball. By all accounts he was a sophisticated man who felt comfortable with whites and who in turn made an excellent impression on most whites he encountered. Yet after he had retired from baseball and become a writer, publisher, and African-American leader, Walker's solution to the problem of racism in America was the separation of the races.

Fowler's time in organized baseball taught him that what whites wanted from African-American athletes was not the skill, dignity, and professionalism that Sol White was so concerned with, but a minstrel-type show. Walker's firsthand experience with integrated baseball taught him that the best hope for

African Americans was to emigrate from the United States to Africa. "Instead of improving [race relations]," Walker wrote in his 1908 book, "we are experiencing the development of a real caste spirit in the United States." For the future, he continued, America offers African Americans "nothing but failure and disappointment."

JIM CROW WINS

Cap Anson Gets the Save

With ten African Americans playing in organized baseball—eight of them in the International League—Sol White called 1887 "a banner year for colored talent in the white leagues." But it was also the year that the tide in baseball began to turn back in the direction of the color line. African Americans in white baseball had always traveled a rocky road. They were subjected to hostility from teammates, racial discrimination by their teams, and terrible verbal abuse from fans and the press. What made 1887 different was the reaction of baseball's power structure to these things. Where in the past individual clubs for the most part had made their own decisions about whether to hire African Americans and handled any racial problems themselves, in 1887 the organized baseball establishment seems to have decided that integration was a failed experiment and that it had to go.

Reestablishing the color line required some delicacy. Baseball as a professional sport was in the business of selling competition. Fans who bought tickets expected to see the best teams and best players doing everything they could to win. By refusing to hire competent African Americans, organized baseball leagues and teams failed to do this, and lowered the level of competition. Also, organized baseball was selling itself as America's national game. Baseball was supposed to reflect American values, such as fairness, honesty, and democracy. Racism did not belong on the list. This explains why organized baseball moved so slowly and cautiously to rid itself of African-American players once the decision had been made in 1887. After the International League showed the way, the other white professional leagues one by one drew the color line. It took a full decade, but by the late 1890s every African-American player had been driven out of organized baseball.

There was an unusually high number of unpleasant racial incidents in the International League in 1887, many of them involving the Syracuse Stars. A power-hitting catcher named Dick Male was released by the Stars after he was discovered to be the light-skinned African-American player Richard Johnson (also known as Dick Noyle and Dick Neale) attempting to pass as white. A clique of ex–Southern League players on the Stars tried their best to make nineteen-year-old African-American pitcher Robert Higgins look bad by playing poorly behind him. In one game, they overdid it and lost 28–8 on a series of outlandish errors. Two white players on the Stars, pitcher Doug Crothers from St. Louis and outfielder Harry Simon from Utica, New York, refused to pose with Higgins for the team picture. Crothers and Stars manager Joe Simmons got into a fistfight over the issue.

Binghamton players gave an African-American pitcher named Renfroe the same treatment that Syracuse gave Higgins; he and Bud Fowler were

The Syracuse Stars of the International League were involved in a number of racial incidents in 1887.

released in midseason. IL umpire Billy Hoover caused a stir by admitting in an Oswego newspaper that he would "always decide against a team employing a colored player, on a close point." During a game between Buffalo and Toronto, Toronto fans chanted "Kill the nigger!" at Frank Grant. There was even a backlash in parts of the normally liberal press. "How far will this mania for engaging colored players go?" sneered the *Sporting Life.* "At the present rate of progress the International League may ere many moons change its name to the 'Colored League.' "

One particular racial incident, however, attracted national attention and came to symbolize the spirit of the 1887 season. It occurred on July 14 in Newark, New Jersey. A large crowd of three thousand fans had turned out for an afternoon exhibition game between the home team, the International League's Newark Little Giants, and the National League's Chicago White Stockings. In the 1880s, as in the 1870s, in-season exhibition games commonly provided a way for clubs to make extra income or defray traveling expenses incurred during road trips. Even though African Americans were unofficially barred from the major leagues, it was not at all uncommon for such exhibition games to feature integrated minor-league teams or African-American independent teams.

"Cap" Anson's legendary Chicago White Stockings—or Colts, as they were also called—drew big crowds everywhere they went. The team would go on to finish third that year, six and a half games behind Detroit, but the White Stockings were considered the class of the league. Their leader, player-manager Anson, was baseball's biggest star.

The White Stockings carried an aura in the last quarter of the nineteenth century that can be compared only to that of the New York Yankees in the middle decades of the twentieth. After winning its first National League pennant in 1876 behind Anson and pitcher Al Spalding, the team built a dynasty that won five pennants in seven seasons from 1880 to 1886. The Chicago lineup was studded with such stars as catcher King Kelly; pitchers Larry Corcoran, Fred Goldsmith, and John Clarkson; second baseman Fred Pfeffer; and a trio of speedy "colts" in the outfield: George Gore, Abner Dalrymple, and Billy Sunday—the future evangelist. At first base was the great Anson himself. A .300-hitter for each of the previous sixteen major-league seasons, in 1887 the thirty-five-year-old Anson was far from over the hill. For the past two seasons combined Anson had hit a combined 70 doubles, 18 triples, and 17 home runs, and had driven in 255 runs in only 237 games!

The other drawing card that day was Newark's popular African-American battery of George Stovey and Fleet Walker. As it turned out, however, the Newark fans were cheated of the advertised matchup between Stovey, the IL's best pitcher, and Anson, the NL's best hitter. Before the game, Anson told Newark management that he would pull his team from the field unless they replaced the African Americans with white players. Facing three thousand ticket refunds, Newark agreed. Stovey and Walker were benched, and the team announced in the press that Stovey had become too ill to play. The real story soon came out. A Toronto newspaper reported that "[Newark manager Charlie] Hackett intended putting Stovey in the box against the Chicagos, but Anson objected to his playing on account of his color."

This incident is important not because it shows that many white players in the 1880s were racists; racists had never been in short supply in baseball. Neither was it news that Cap Anson tried to intimidate an opposing team into benching an African-American player. Anson had tried this at least once before, in 1883, and he would try it again in 1888. What was new this time was that Anson got away with it.

When the Stovey-Walker benching is compared to the other two known incidents involving Anson, it becomes clear that 1887 was a turning point. In 1883 the White Stockings were playing an exhibition game against Toledo's minor league team. Fleet Walker was Toledo's regular catcher. Anson threatened to cancel the game if an African American appeared on the field, but Toledo stood tall and insisted that Walker stay in the lineup. Not only did Anson play the game against Walker, but he was made fun of in the press. The *Sporting Life* later revealed that "the joke of the affair was that up to the time Anson made his 'bluff' the Toledo people had no intention of catching Walker, who was laid up with a sore hand, but when Anson said he wouldn't play with Walker, the Toledo people made up their minds that Walker would catch or there wouldn't be any game." The second time Anson tried to have an African-American player removed— the 1887 Stovey-Walker incident—he succeeded, but not without creating a controversy.

In 1888, Anson tried for a third time to have an African-American player taken out of the lineup. Again Fleet Walker was involved. The White Stockings' opponent was Syracuse, Walker's new club. Syracuse complied with Anson's request and benched him without complaint. What had been an outrage to many a year earlier, however, was considered so unremarkable in 1888 that only one newspaper, the African-American *Indianapolis World,* made any mention of it at all.

CAP ANSON

Adrian Constantine "Cap" Anson was a towering figure both in physique—at six feet tall and 227 pounds, he was one of the largest men in the game—and in his impact on the game of baseball.

No player until Babe Ruth in the 1920s was as closely identified with a team and a league as was Anson with the Chicago White Stockings and the National League. After five years in the NA, where he batted .352, Anson signed with Chicago in William Hulbert's new major league in 1876. He stayed with Chicago for twenty-two seasons, long enough to become known by three different nicknames: "Baby," because of his constant complaining over umpiring calls as a young man; "Cap," for captain, after he took over as Chicago player-manager in 1879; and finally, "Pop," when he was in his late thirties. By the time he retired at age forty-five, the idea of the Chicago White Stockings without Pop Anson was so unimaginable that the team became known for a while as the "Orphans."

In spite of his size, Anson employed the singles-oriented style of batting popular in the 1870s and early 1880s. Choking up or holding the bat with the hands a few inches apart, Anson would slap or poke the ball softly past the infielders. Most of his extra-base hits came on line-drives placed between the outfielders rather than great wallops in the style of today's power-hitters. He batted .329 in his two decades plus in the NL, including a .399 mark in 1881 and .388 in 1894, when he was forty-two. He was the first man ever to collect three thousand career major-league hits.

Without question Anson was one of the biggest single factors in the popularity and success of the National League. He was the idol of nineteenth-century boys everywhere and his face was as familiar to most Americans as Abraham Lincoln's. The hundreds of exhibition games Anson's team played against local teams across the country did much to promote the NL and baseball as a whole. In his autobiography, the great twentieth-century manager Connie Mack described the excitement when Anson came to Mack's hometown of East Brookfield, Massachusetts. "It was a bigger event to us than the inauguration of a President," Mack remembered, "We cheered ourselves hoarse as Pop Anson and his Colts trotted onto our sandlot. What a glorious sight it was!"[1]

Anson's bluff Western style, however, alienated many inside baseball. The dignified Easterner Henry

Chadwick called him "an acknowledged rough." Born in the primitive frontier town of Marshalltown, Iowa, and raised among the Pottawatomie Indians, he was a stern taskmaster as a manager, demanding from his players total dedication to his own personal principles of hard work, discipline, and clean living. Like Sol White, he was very concerned with elevating the standards and status of his profession, and this may provide a clue to why he campaigned so fiercely for the color line in baseball. Many people from Sol White's time until today have searched for evidence of some unusually strong racial prejudice or unpleasant personal experience that might explain Anson's attitude toward African-American ballplayers. They often cite a few passages in Anson's 1900 autobiography, *A Ballplayer's Career,* in which Anson refers to a baseball mascot named Clarence Duval as a "coon" or "no-account nigger." But ugly slurs like these were as commonplace in Anson's time as the presence of Duval and other African-American mascots, who were kept around white baseball teams for the amusement of players or as a kind of good luck charm, since rubbing an African American's head was considered by many whites to be good luck. The official baseball guides of the 1880s regularly called African-American players "coons."

A better place to look for Anson's motivation may be in the "culture of professionalism" that was on the rise in late nineteenth-century America. At this time, lawyers, doctors, and other professionals began to organize to improve their economic and social status. According to historian Jules Tygiel, such groups "formed organizations, established standards of performance, and erected barriers to entry. Racial and ethnic exclusion often constituted a means to define the distinctiveness of a given profession."[2] In other words, Anson may have urged the exclusion of African

*"Cap" Anson (left), an influential proponent of
segregation in baseball, and Rube Foster (right),
the father of the Negro Leagues.*

Americans for the same reason that he wanted to exclude drunks and criminals—because he felt that their
low social standing lowered the prestige of his profession. This kind of thinking was typical of a time
when many middle-class institutions and professions
considered the exclusion of African Americans, Irish
Americans, Catholics, and Jews to be a mark of prestige.

Not a very intelligent man, Anson had a rugged
integrity and stuck stubbornly to what he thought
was right. In 1890 he was one of the few big-name

players not to join in the Player's League revolt, an early baseball union action. He became very unpopular among his fellow players as a result. In spite of Anson's loyalty to management, his relationship with his boss, Al Spalding—millionaire sporting goods manufacturer, former player, and Chicago White Stockings owner—was a stormy one. After he retired, Anson became very bitter over being cheated of money that he felt Spalding owed him. When Spalding responded by trying to arrange a benefit to raise money for Anson's retirement, Anson angrily and publicly refused. "I refuse to accept anything in the shape of a gift," he declared. "The public owes me nothing."

In the six short years from 1883 to 1888, baseball's racial climate changed radically. According to Sol White, Cap Anson was the main reason. White writes in his 1907 book:

> "Anson, with all the venom of a hate which would be worthy of a Tilliman or a Vardaman [two prominent white-supremacist Southern politicians] of the present day, made strenuous and fruitful opposition to any proposition looking to the admittance of a colored man into the National League. Just why Adrian Anson, manager and captain of the Chicago National League club, was so strongly opposed to colored players on white teams cannot be explained. His repugnant feeling, shown at every opportunity, toward colored ballplayers, was a source of comment throughout every league in the country and his opposition, with his great popularity and power in baseball circles, hastened the exclusion of the black man from the white leagues."[3]

The idea of Anson as the prime mover behind the drawing of the color line in the late 1880s has had a long life in the folk history of baseball and in the African-American press. In its obituary of Anson in 1922 the *Chicago Defender,* a prominent African-American newspaper, wrote that Anson "sow[ed] his seeds of prejudice" among "ignorant" fellow ballplayers by convincing them to refuse to play against African Americans, Native Americans, Asians, and other minority players. The *Defender* also claimed that Anson would not allow Anson's Colts, a semipro team he promoted after his retirement from the National League, to play against any of Chicago's African-American independent teams.

This last charge is not true. Anson's Colts played many times against African-American clubs; Rube Foster's famous Leland Giants of the otherwise white City League of Chicago were a frequent opponent. A photograph survives that shows Anson and Foster in a friendly pose. Furthermore, it is doubtful that Cap Anson could have been solely, or even primarily, responsible for the return of the color line in every part of organized baseball, in every part of the country. On the same July day in 1887 that Anson bullied Newark into benching Stovey and Walker, an event was taking place in a boardroom in Buffalo that had far more ominous implications for the future of African Americans on white professional teams than all of the racial incidents in baseball clubhouses, grandstands, or playing fields put together.

The board of directors of the International League was meeting at the Genesee House, a Buffalo hotel, the announced reason for the meeting was to settle the financial affairs of a bankrupt IL franchise. Whether that was the real reason or a cover, the *Sporting Life* reported the next day that the directors had held a private meeting on July 14, 1887, in which the subject of African-American players was discussed. "Several representatives declared," the story reads, "that many of the best players in the league were anxious to leave on account of the colored element, and the board finally directed Secretary White to approve no more contracts with colored men." With this directive the IL took a step that no other baseball organization since the NABBP in 1867 had dared. For the first time in twenty years—and for the first time ever in professional baseball—the baseball color line had been drawn in black and white.

According to baseball historian Jerry Malloy, the IL directors voted six to four in favor of the ban. The vote count suggests that opposition from racist players may not have been the real reason for the directors' decision to exclude African Americans. The six clubs without an African-American player voted in favor of the contract ban; the four clubs that had African-American players—Buffalo, Oswego, Newark, and Syracuse—voted against it. It was these four clubs, of course, that had experienced most of the clubhouse conflicts and other racial problems that the ban was supposedly addressing.

Nineteenth-century team owners and league officials often used the racist feelings of players such as Anson to justify the Jim Crow policies of organized baseball. But there is good reason to suspect that this was nothing but an excuse. After all, this was a time when baseball owners treated their players as if they were private property. The 1880s and 1890s were a historic low point in salaries, rights, and influence of the players on the management of the game. During this period the owners imposed a strict salary limit of $2,500 on all players; in 1887 they made the hated reserve clause part of every player's contract. These and other repressive, high-handed measures by the owners drove the exploited major-league players, led by New York Giants shortstop John Montgomery Ward, to form the first sports union in the late 1880s. In 1890, after the owners refused to bargain in good faith with the player's union, the players broke away from organized baseball to form their own major league. Ward's Player's League failed after one season. With the player's union now broken, the owners reimposed the reserve clause and established a new salary limit of $2,400 per year. Albert Spalding and the other arrogant nineteenth-century baseball owners made no secret of the fact that they did not care what the players thought about anything. Why then would they have cared how players felt about playing with African Americans?

Most newspapers, and certainly most of those located in cities with popular African-American stars, blasted the IL's new Jim Crow policy. The *Binghamton Daily Leader* stated that "the International League made a monkey out of itself when it undertook to draw the color line." The *Syracuse Standard* called the ban a "shameful regulation." The *Newark Daily Journal* said that "It is safe to say that Moses F. Walker is mentally and morally the equal of any director who voted for the resolution." Most eloquent of all was the *Newark Call,* which thundered:

If anywhere in this world the social barriers are broken down it is on the ball field. There many men of low birth and poor breeding are the idols of the rich and cultured; the best man is he who plays best. Even men of churlish dispositions and coarse hues are tolerated on the field. In view of these facts the objection to colored men is ridiculous. If social distinctions are made, half the players in the country will be shut out. Better make character and per-

sonal habits the test. Weed out the toughs and intemperate men first, and then it may be in order to draw the color line.[4]

Over the following winter, the IL reacted to this barrage of criticism with a smoke screen. Off the record, each club was allowed a quota of two African Americans for 1888, but it was understood that no more would be added in the future. Four of the eight African Americans who had played in the IL in 1887—Johnson, Fowler, Renfroe, and a man named Pointter—were released during the season and not re-signed. Of the four who finished the season and who would have been excluded under the original version of the ban, Frank Grant played one more season with Buffalo, although he was moved to the outfield because of repeated spikings, and Fleet Walker moved from Newark to Syracuse. Tired of being let down and humiliated by his own teammates, pitcher Robert Higgins quit the Stars in August of 1888 and returned to his job as a barber in Memphis, Tennessee. By 1889 only Walker was left. A year later he was gone, too. The IL was now completely white.

Other minor leagues followed the International League's lead. They learned quickly that it was much less trouble to draw the color line in secret. That way they could avoid the embarrassment of being criticized by the press and having to defend their racist actions in public. During the Winter of 1887–1888 the Ohio State League publicly repealed "the law permitting colored men to sign." Fleet Walker's brother Welday, who had played in 1887 for Akron in the Ohio State League, sent an open letter to league president W. H. McDermitt, expressing his outrage. In it he wrote:

The law is a disgrace to the present age and reflects very much upon the intelligence of your

*last meeting, and casts derision at the laws of
Ohio—the voice of the people—that says all
men are created equal. I would suggest that
your honorable body, in case that black law is
not repealed, pass one making it criminal for a
colored man or woman to be found on a ball
ground. There is now the same accommoda-
tion made for the colored patron of the game
as the white, and the same provision and dis-
pensation is made for the money of both of
them that finds its way into the coffers of the
various clubs.*[5]

Walker's letter shamed the Ohio State League into
officially rescinding its color line policy. The number
of African-American players in the league, however,
dropped from three in 1887 to zero the following year.
Nothing now could change the racial course of organized baseball. In the future, professional leagues
would be more careful not to make their racial policy
in public, but they drew the color line just the same.

While individual African-American players were
being weeded out of the high minors and the top
Eastern leagues during 1887, 1888, and 1889, Bud
Fowler, Richard Johnson, Sol White, and a few others
continued to move back and forth between African-
American independent teams and organized baseball
in the relatively more liberal West. For a short time
they stayed one step ahead of the advancing color line,
playing in small towns like Galesburg, Peoria, and
Fort Wayne in leagues like the Central Interstate
League, the Illinois-Iowa League, and the Western
Interstate League.

There was one exception to the overall trend in
baseball toward the color line. A new form of integration was tried by a few lower minor leagues that
briefly admitted whole African-American teams. In

1889 two entire independent African-American teams, the New York Gorhams and the Cuban Giants, were hired to represent Philadelphia, Pennsylvania, and Trenton, New Jersey, respectively, in the Middle States League. The Cuban Giants featured George Stovey, Frank Grant, Jack Frye, and Sol White; not surprisingly, they came within a whisker of winning the Middle States League pennant over a strong Harrisburg, Pennsylvania, team. A year later the Middle States League reorganized as the Eastern Interstate League. When that league folded in the middle of the 1890 season, the Cuban Giants, this time representing York, Pennsylvania, were in first place. In 1891 the Cuban Giants moved again, to Ansonia, Connecticut, in the Connecticut State League. Once again, before the end of the season, the Connecticut State League went out of business.

The final African-American team to play in a white league was an obscure outfit called the Acme Colored Giants, which played part of the 1898 season in Celeron, New York, in the Oil and Iron League. That was the end of this integration experiment, although to call it integration may be an exaggeration. It is probably more accurate to view this as an extension of the established custom of white clubs and African-American clubs playing exhibition games outside the organized baseball structure.

The last appearances by African Americans in the white minors occurred far outside the baseball mainstream, in small-time leagues in Kansas and Michigan. In the middle 1890s some of Bud Fowler's Page Fence Giants played briefly for Adrian, Michigan, in the Michigan State League. Adrian was in a tight pennant race and borrowed Bud Fowler and a few of his players to strengthen the team late in the season. Ironically, Adrian, Michigan, is the same town that Cap Anson's father, who had grown up in Michigan, named his son after.

The very last African-American player in nineteenth-century organized baseball was Bert Jones. Nicknamed the "Yellow Kid" after the first popular newspaper comic-strip character, Jones was a fireballing left-handed pitcher who played for Atchison in the Kansas State League in 1897 and 1898. A local newspaper reported that a new team member "from Missouri" said that he would "have nothing to do with a Cuban." Bert Jones was released at about the same time. The next African American to play in organized baseball would be Jackie Robinson, who signed with Montreal in the International League in 1946. For the forty-eight years in between, Jim Crow reigned supreme over the national game.

What happened in baseball in the late 1880s and 1890s was happening in the rest of American society as well. White supremacism—the philosophy that whites are inherently superior to African Americans, moved back into the political mainstream hand in hand with its partner Jim Crow. Once an exclusively Northern phenomenon, Jim Crow laws were adopted and improved upon by Southerners. The first Jim Crow measures in Southern states were aimed at disenfranchising, or taking away the right to vote from, African Americans. Once African Americans were denied the vote, they lost all political power; this in turn made it easier for white supremacists, who gained more and more power over state governments, to pass segregation laws.

The resurgence of white supremacism in the late 19th century had little to do directly with the Civil War, Reconstruction or the KKK. Nor was it only a Southern phenomenon. Instead it was the result of the convergence of a number of new political, economic and philosophical forces that affected every region. A widespread agrarian depression led some people to scapegoat African Americans for the economic hard times. The scientific ideas of evolutionist

Charles Darwin, including the preservation of the species and the survival of the fittest, were popularized and distorted to justify theories of racial or ethnic superiority. For example, a Congregationalist missionary named Josiah Strong advocated American imperialism in a best-selling book, *Our Country*, published in 1885. Strong used Darwinian ideas to argue that God had chosen the Anglo-Saxon race to dominate Native Americans, African Americans, and other races as if they were their "brothers' keeper."

The growing numbers of immigrants from Asia and the Slavic and Mediterranean countries were making many Americans uncomfortable. Jim Crow laws were aimed at Asian Americans on the West Coast. With the support of American labor unions, Congress passed the first restriction on immigration to the United States. Isolationist, anti-Catholic, and anti-immigrant ideas influenced the political scene more and more. Anti-Catholic feeling ran so high that the presidential candidacy of Adm. George Dewey was withdrawn when it became known that his wife was Catholic. In one horrible example of anti-immigrant hysteria, eleven Sicilian immigrants were lynched by a mob in New Orleans in 1891. What one historian called a "cult of Nordicism," or a belief that people of white, northern European stock were inherently superior, swept the country.

On the opposite side of the spectrum from the isolationists, who wanted America to stay out of world politics and foreign wars, were those Americans who saw the United States as the rightful successor to England as the world's next great colonial empire. These ideas made possible the U.S. annexation of Hawaii in 1893 and the Spanish-American War of 1898 and 1899, during which the American military took over Cuba and Puerto Rico. The American Army's invasion of the Philippines and suppression of the independence movement led by Gen. Emilio Aguinaldo were particularly brutal.

These bloody imperialist adventures sapped the moral authority of the North. Southerners Ben "Pitchfork" Tilliman and James K. Vardaman harped on Northern hypocrisy on the floor of the United States Senate. Northerners "no longer denounce the suppression of the Negro vote as it used to be denounced in the Reconstruction days," Senator Vardaman said in 1900. "The necessity of it under the supreme law of self-preservation is candidly recognized." Senator Tilliman added:

> No Republican leader, not even Governor [Theodore] Roosevelt, will now dare to wave the bloody shirt [an abolitionist symbol for the brutality of slavery] and preach a crusade against the South's treatment of the Negro. The North has a bloody shirt of its own. Many thousands of them have been made into shrouds for murdered Filipinos, done to death because they were fighting for liberty."[6]

There was little will left among Northern congressmen to defend the civil rights of African Americans. Regardless of the political realities, the Supreme Court should have been the guardian of rights given to African Americans by the Constitution and the Reconstructionist Congress of the 1860s and 1870s. In the late 1880s and 1890s, however, the court went with the political flow and weakened or destroyed nearly all of those legal protections.

Jim Crow was an old Yankee tradition going way back before the Civil War and the abolitionist movement. Voting rights were not an issue in the pre-war South, where most African Americans were slaves. In the North, of course, African Americans were free and the vote had to be taken away from them by law. This was done in Delaware in 1792, in Kentucky in 1799, in Maryland and in Ohio in 1799, and in New Jersey in 1801. By the start of the Civil War, African Americans had been completely or partially denied the vote in Connecticut, New York, Rhode Island, Pennsylvania, Indiana, Illinois, Michigan, Iowa, Wisconsin, Minnesota and Kansas. In many states, African Americans had to prove that they owned a certain amount of property in order to be able to vote; whites were exempt from this requirement.

According to Richard Kluger in his book *Simple Justice,* "By custom, Negroes were excluded from jury service throughout the North. They were either kept off of or assigned to Jim Crow sections of public conveyances of every sort, from stagecoach to steamboat; most theaters, restaurants, and public lodgings were closed to them, and in those churches that continued to practice interracial worship the black man prayed in pews set aside for him, usually as far aside as possible."[7]

The South borrowed these practices beginning in the late 1880s. Because the Fourteenth and Fifteenth Amendments to the Constitution guaranteed them the equal protection of the law and the right to vote, Southern white supremacist politicians could not simply pass a law taking the vote away from African Americans. Instead, they introduced complicated voting procedures that made it harder and harder for them to vote. South Carolina invented a multiple ballot box system that was so confusing it bewildered most uneducated voters of either race. Voter disenfranchisement techniques were perfected all across the South in the 1890s. Some states began to collect a poll tax; those who could not pay were denied the right to vote.

Literacy tests to determine eligibility to vote were introduced in South Carolina in 1895, Louisiana in

1898, and North Carolina in 1900. These tests were often graded subjectively in order to allow officials to pass illiterate whites. In Mississippi, for instance, a would-be voter had to be able to read and explain a section of the state constitution to the satisfaction of a (usually white) official. The 1898 Louisiana voting law included the original "grandfather clause": any man was automatically qualified to vote whose grandfather had been a registered voter as of January 1, 1867. This effectively restricted the vote to whites, since this date was just before African Americans were given the vote in Louisiana under the First Reconstruction Act.

Disenfranchisement measures did their job. In 1896, for instance, 130,334 African Americans were registered to vote in Louisiana; they formed a strong political force and were a majority in numerous parishes. Eight years later there were only 1,342. "By 1910," writes Kluger, "every Southern state had followed the lead of South Carolina and Mississippi in reducing the black man to a political cipher."

The disappearance of African-American voting power led to further abuses. The number of African-American mayors, police chiefs, judges and legislators in the South declined drastically. The 1890s saw an increase in aggression against African Americans, including a staggering outbreak of lynchings. Stricter segregation laws were passed. Intended not only to separate the races but to humiliate and intimidate African Americans, these laws were a form of aggression as well. The first segregation laws applied only to trains, streetcars, and other public transportation; they required that Jim Crow cars be provided so that African Americans and whites would travel separately. Although such laws were enacted by many Southern states, the first law to be challenged in the federal courts was that of Louisiana, a state with a longstanding and sizeable free African-American community and a relatively liberal racial atmosphere. In the case of *Plessy* v. *Ferguson,* lawyers for a man who had been ejected from a "white" railroad car argued that the Louisiana law was unconstitutional under the Fourteenth Amendment, which guaranteed all citizens the equal protection of the law.

In 1896 the Supreme Court decided *Plessy* v. *Ferguson.* It upheld the segregation law and established the doctrine known as "separate but equal." Speaking for the majority of the court, Justice Henry Billings Brown, a Northerner from Massachusetts, argued, with *Alice in Wonderland* logic,

> *We consider the underlying fallacy of the plaintiff's argument to consist in the assumption that the enforced separation of the two races stamps the colored race with a badge of inferiority. If this be so, it is not by reason of anything found in the act, but solely because the colored race chooses to put that construction upon it.*[8]

In his dissenting opinion, Justice John Marshall Harlan, a former slaveholder from Kentucky, stated the obvious. "Everyone knows," he wrote, that the law's purpose is "to exclude colored people from coaches occupied by or assigned to white persons. . . . The thin disguise of 'equal' accommodations for passengers in railroad coaches will not mislead anyone, nor atone for the wrong this day done."[9]

The Supreme Court followed the thinking of Justice Brown during the 1890s and early 1900s. In one decision after another, the legal basis of Reconstruction was undone, and segregated railroad cars were followed by Jim Crow rest rooms, restaurants, hotels, and water fountains. Within only a few years, it seemed to most people that this was the way

American life always had been and the way it always had to be. Both in the North and in the South it was quickly forgotten that once, in the words of C. Vann Woodward, there had been a time when "[a]lternatives were still open and real choices had to be made."

In 1900, only two years after the last African-American ballplayer had been banished from organized baseball, the *Richmond Times* proclaimed, "God Almighty drew the color line and it cannot be obliterated. The Negro must stay on his side of the line and the white man must stay on his side."

WAR PAINT AND FEATHERS

Jim Crow and Chief Tokohama

America progressed more in the two decades between 1900 and 1920 than it had in some centuries. In almost every area of life, from baseball to architecture to transportation to public health to politics, this was a time of rapid and sometimes violent change.

The America of the year 1900 was a rural, agricultural nation whose economy depended on farming and the railroads. There were no airplanes, automobiles, or highways. Because of poor sanitation and such diseases as yellow fever, scarlet fever, diphtheria, and malaria, the average person lived to be only forty-nine years old. Many children in cities and mill towns worked long hours in grim factories. In most places women could not vote. The tallest building in downtown New York City was the spire of the century-old Trinity Church.

By 1920, America had become much more like the America that we know today. Plastic, movies, and the airplane were invented. Factory-made cigarettes became popular and replaced handmade cigars, snuff, and chewing tobacco. Originally a luxury item for the very rich, automobiles were mass-produced and made affordable for the middle class by Henry Ford. The construction of the first interstate highways stimulated a wave of road building. The first great skyscrapers were built in Chicago and New York.

Ragtime music, a type of jazz created by African Americans, was popularized for white audiences by Irving Berlin, while a succession of "animal dance" crazes, including the fox-trot, turkey trot, and bunny hug, swept the country. The Nineteenth Amendment guaranteed women the right to vote, and child labor laws were passed. The federal government introduced the income tax and the forty-hour workweek became the rule. By 1920, for the first time in history, more than 50 percent of Americans lived in cities, and the average life expectancy reached fifty-four.

Not all of the changes of the 1900s and 1910s, however, were positive. This was an era of great political and social upheaval. An economic recession called the "Panic of '07" left many people trapped in poverty. The first great urban slums appeared. The tremendous power of "trusts," or large business monopolies, manipulated prices and exploited workers and consumers, producing an atmosphere of greed and corruption. Nearly every type of big business was controlled by trusts; there was an oil trust, a coal trust, and a beef trust. Wealth became more and more concentrated in the hands of a few multimillionaires and "robber barons."

The years just before World War I brought a backlash against these trends in the form of socialist, communist, and even anarchist movements. Radical political groups and labor unions clashed violently with the police. Assassins killed President William McKinley and capitalist J. Pierpont Morgan; another wounded President Teddy Roosevelt. In 1919 anarchists mailed letter bombs to thirty prominent businessmen and politicians. There was even a backlash against the backlash. Right-wing U.S. Attorney

General A. Mitchell Palmer initiated a campaign of persecution and terror that was nicknamed the "Red Scare." Aimed mainly at leftist politicians and African Americans such as the activist poet Claude McKay, the Red Scare of 1919 foreshadowed the anti-communist hysteria of the McCarthy era of the 1950s.

Continuing a trend from the 1890s, the United States threw its military weight around in Latin America. American soldiers landed in Cuba in 1906 and 1912, Honduras in 1907, Haiti and the Dominican Republic in 1916, and Mexico in 1910. Panama was taken away from Colombia by force so that the Panama Canal could be built.

Baseball also changed and modernized. In 1900 there was only one major league, the National League, with eight teams playing in seven cities in only six states. There were no games broadcast on the radio and no World Series. Ballparks were slapdash wooden structures that burned down with regularity. On the field, baseball was dominated by second-generation Irish Americans who played a tough style of baseball featuring beanballs, fistfighting, and intimidation of opponents and officials. It was not unknown for turn-of-the-century umpires to carry pistols while on duty.

In 1901 the American League, based in the Midwest, entered the scene, offering what its president, Ban Johnson, called "clean baseball." This meant more discipline and respect for umpires, and less of the rowdiness that the National League had become known for in the 1890s. Beginning in 1903 the two leagues began to play a postseason World Series (the beginning of the modern World Series). The two-league, sixteen-team format proved so successful it remained in place for fifty years. There was not a single expansion, structural change, or franchise shift in major league baseball until the Boston Braves moved to Milwaukee in 1953. Starting in 1909 with Philadelphia's Shibe Park and continuing through the 1910s, baseball clubs built the first generation of beautiful and permanent concrete and steel ballparks, including three beloved parks that still stand today—Wrigley Field, Fenway Park, and Tiger Stadium.

Like American society, baseball in the 1910s had a grim side. The baseball monopoly may not have been as profitable as the big business monopolies, but it was just as greedy and exploitive. Most players were poorly paid and treated like indentured servants. Dozens of them were caught fixing games for gamblers and were thrown out of the game for life. After rising in the 1900s, attendance fell throughout the 1910s. Baseball writer and editor Francis Richter attributed this to "squabbles over excessive player salaries . . . the mercenary spirit displayed by the players . . . political unrest and revolution in the nation . . . the constant harassment and depression of the country's big and little businesses. . . ."[1]

These years also saw change of a sort in race relations. Unfortunately, it was change in the direction of more segregation and racial hatred. Jim Crow reached its absolute peak in American history between 1900 and 1920. This was especially true in the South, which missed out on such positive trends of the time as immigration and urban growth. As a result, the South became more and more culturally and economically isolated. The Ku Klux Klan revived in 1915 in Georgia and rode virtually unchallenged by the federal government. Following the election victory of a white supremacist politician in Atlanta in 1906, white mobs rioted for four days, looting, burning, and attacking African Americans. Across the South, Jim Crow laws were refined and extended to cover the most trivial activities. North Carolina and Virginia, for instance, outlawed fraternal organizations that permitted members of different races to call each other "brother." Other towns, cities, and states passed laws requiring separate public elevators for whites and African Americans and separate bibles for witnesses to swear on in court. Birmingham, Alabama, outlawed interracial checkers games, even in private homes.

Of course, neither the KKK nor Jim Crow was unknown in the North. At its peak in the 1920s, the KKK had more members outside the South than inside. Some major league ballplayers were KKK members, among them future Hall of Famers Rogers Hornsby, Ty Cobb, and Tris Speaker. The first laws aimed at segregating city neighborhoods appeared in Baltimore in 1910. After these laws were declared unconstitutional by the Supreme Court in 1917, Northerners resorted to other techniques. They used "gentleman's agreements" and invented the restrictive covenant, which forced the buyer of a property to promise not to sell it in the future to an African American or a member of another minority group, such as Jews.

World War I shook up the Northern racial picture in many ways. Adding to a migration that had begun in 1915 and 1916, thousands of African Americans came north to work in factories that were busily producing war-related products. Like many whites, these workers believed American war propaganda that portrayed the war against the Germans as a battle for democracy and human rights.

For this reason and because they were doing their part in the war effort—360,000 African Americans served in the military during World War I—African Americans hoped to find equality and fairer treatment in the North in the postwar years. But when the war ended and the soldiers came home, they were bitterly disappointed. In a terrible white protest against the rapidly growing African-American presence in the North, rioting broke out in 1919 in twenty-five cities across the country. Known collectively as the "Red Summer," these were the bloodiest race riots in American history. As in the Atlanta riot of 1906, nearly all of the violence was done by whites to African Americans. The Chicago riot was the worst. Mobs took over that city for several days, beating, robbing, and looting. A total of seventy African Americans were killed in all of the riots. Some died wearing the military uniforms in which they had served their country.

The riots of 1919 had a direct impact on baseball. Throughout the 1900s and 1910s, organized baseball remained the same Jim Crow, Northeastern institution that it had become in the 1890s. Nothing much had changed for most African-American ballplayers since the days of Cap Anson. They remained outside organized baseball, playing for independent, barnstorming African-American clubs. They played challenge matches against each other or against white clubs, and an informal world championship series each fall. But Sol White, Rube Foster, and other African-American baseball men clung to a hope that the integration of the 1880s would return someday and that African Americans would once again be able to cross the color line.

The year 1919 changed all that. The riots forced White, Foster, and the others to realize that Jim Crow was here to stay for a long time. African-American baseball needed to develop its own stable leagues in order to survive until the next thaw in American race relations. In the phrase that Rube Foster made into his personal motto: "[We] have to be ready when the time comes for integration."

In 1920 Foster organized eight Midwestern African-American teams into the Negro National

League (NNL). One of the teams was Foster's Chicago powerhouse, the Chicago American Giants, which went on to win the NNL's first pennant. The NNL was a financial success, often drawing major-league-sized Sunday afternoon crowds of 8,000 in the larger cities. In 1923 a second Negro League was born, the Eastern Colored League (ECL), and a little later the two leagues began to meet in annual world series and all-star games. The sport of professional baseball was now a perfect mirror of American society. There was one baseball world for whites and another—parallel but completely separate—for African Americans.

The drawing of the baseball color line for good in 1898 did not mean that the color line went unchallenged, or that everyone within organized baseball accepted it. The 1900s began with an attempt to break the color line by John McGraw, manager of the AL Baltimore Orioles. Once a star third baseman with the down and dirty NL Baltimore Orioles of the 1890s, McGraw was much more interested in winning than in racial politics. When McGraw saw a player who could help him win in the major leagues, he went after him.

One March day in 1901 in Hot Springs, Arkansas, where the Orioles conducted their spring training, McGraw was watching the bellboys from the Eastland Hotel playing a pickup baseball game. McGraw was impressed by an African-American second baseman named Charlie Grant. Grant had grown up in a German neighborhood of Cincinnati—according to historian Lee Allen, Grant spoke fluent German—and was well known as a player there and in Chicago, where he had played with the African-American Columbia Giants. McGraw approached Grant and offered him a job with the Orioles. As Allen tells the story, McGraw was looking at a map in the hotel lobby

Charlie Grant. At first, the press believed that the second baseman was a Native American.

and called Grant over to him. "Charlie," he said, "I've been trying to think of some way to sign you for the Baltimore club and I think I've got it. On this map there's a creek called Tokohama. That's going to be your name from now on, Charlie Tokohama, and you're a full-blooded Cherokee."[2]

This was not the first time since Fleet Walker played with AA Toledo that a major league team had tried to sign an African American. In 1887, the year of the famous Cap Anson incident in Newark, New York

Giants manager John Montgomery Ward had tried to bring pitcher George Stovey to New York to play in the National League. This is the same Ward who later led the Player's League revolt and who fought for player's rights as a player, as a manager, and—in his post-playing days—as an activist lawyer. Ward saw a parallel between the situations of professional ballplayers and African-American slaves. He wrote a controversial magazine article called "Is the Ballplayer a Chattel [a piece of property]"? and often compared the reserve clause to the infamous Fugitive Slave Act, an 1850 law that required Northern states to return runaway slaves to their former owners. According to Sol White, "arrangements were about completed for [Stovey's] transfer from the Newark club, when a howl was heard from Chicago to New York." The howl was from Cap Anson, and whether because of Anson's protest or not, Stovey never appeared in a Giants uniform.

Charlie Grant had sharp features and straight, jet-black hair. In the beginning, the press believed that he was a Native American. But before the season opened, the secret got out. Legend has it that African-American fans gave Grant away by cheering him a little too enthusiastically during an exhibition game in Chicago. Whether this is true or not, it was Chicago White Sox owner Charles Comiskey who publicly spoke out against Grant, saying:

> I'm not going to stand for McGraw bringing in an Indian on the Baltimore team. If Muggsy [McGraw's nickname] really keeps this Indian, I will get a Chinaman of my acquaintance and put him on third. Somebody told me that the Cherokee of McGraw's is really Grant, the crack Negro second baseman from Cincinnati, fixed up with war paint and a bunch of feathers.[3]

It is interesting that Comiskey, who was known to be relatively open-minded about race, is not opposing the principle of African Americans on white teams so much as he is complaining that McGraw is taking unfair advantage by drawing from a forbidden source of talent. In any case, after this incident McGraw tried to prop up Grant's fictitious family history with more lies, but it was too late. Just before the start of the 1901 season the *Sporting Life* reported that "Tokohama, the Cherokee Indian, will play with the Columbia Giants, of Chicago, again this season."

JOHN McGRAW

John McGraw was born in upstate New York, the son of an Irish immigrant railroad worker. He survived a brutal childhood—including beatings from his father and the deaths of his mother and several brothers and sisters from diphtheria—by turning his anger and aggressiveness toward opponents on the baseball field.

At age eighteen, McGraw was starring at third base for Ned Hanlon's Baltimore Orioles, an NL dynasty of the mid-1890s. A run-scoring machine, McGraw batted .334 for his career, led the NL twice in walks, and stole 436 bases. McGraw came into his own as manager of the New York Giants from 1902 to 1932. The winner of ten pennants and three World Series, he is considered, along with fellow Irish American Connie Mack, one of the two dominant baseball figures of the early twentieth century. To the end McGraw remained a fiery, even abusive, competitor and baiter of umpires and league officials. "The main idea," he liked to say after one of his many suspensions for fighting or swearing at an umpire, "is to win." Off the field, however, he was kind and generous, and formed strong friendships with apparent personality opposites like the gentlemanly, college-educated Christy Mathewson. Few baseball men of his era had as many friends in the game as McGraw; and in those days before professional baseball scouting, McGraw used this vast network to keep the Giants well supplied with talent.

McGraw grew up in a time of great discrimination against the Irish in America. Many professions were completely closed to Irish Americans. (In others, including baseball, Irish Americans were encouraged to drop the *O'* or *Mc* prefixes from their last names in order to make them seem English.) Perhaps for this reason, McGraw was unusually sympathetic to players from disliked minority groups. He signed Native American players, including outfielder Jim Thorpe and catcher Chief Meyers, at a time when many fans took them for African Americans trying to pass. Meyers often had to put up with fans yelling "Nigger!" during games. There is little question that African Americans would have been allowed to play in the majors if it had been up to McGraw. Not only did he try to sign Charlie Grant, but he went after dark-skinned Cuban pitcher Jose Mendez. Rumor had it that he also tried to sign William Matthews, an African American from the Harvard baseball team. In later years, he entertained the idea of sneaking the great Negro League outfielder Oscar Charleston and

Oscar Charleston.
John McGraw of
the Baltimore Orioles
tried to sign this great
Negro League outfielder
by disguising him as a
Cuban immigrant.

at least one other player into the NL by disguising them as Cuban immigrants. In the case of Mendez, it was reported at the time that McGraw was "prevented by fellow National League executives from importing the Cuban Negro star." After his death, McGraw's wife revealed that he had kept a running list of African-American players that he considered good prospects in case he ever got the opportunity to sign them.

Responding to the hardening of racial attitudes in American society in the 1900s and 1910s, baseball maintained a facade of strict segregation. Not only were African Americans kept out of organized baseball, but in the racially tense atmosphere of the time, dark-skinned players were often accused of "passing." Sometimes the accusation proved to be false, as with George Treadway in the 1890s or Sandy Nava in the 1880s. Other times, it was true. Part-Native American pitcher Jimmy Claxton played briefly for Oakland in 1916 in the minor Pacific Coast League—before he was discovered to be part-African American, too. He appeared on a baseball card before being booted out of organized baseball. Some African-American players probably did manage to pass undetected. As one sportswriter put it in the early 1940s, "It is no secret that players of suspected Negro parentage have appeared in big league games."

Further confusing the racial picture in the 1900s and 1910s were the new phenomena of winter ball and the arrival of Cuban ballplayers in the major leagues. Ironically, these problems might never have come up if it were not for the emergence of American imperialism, which led the United States to invade and then establish a quasi-protectorate over the baseball-playing island of Cuba. The quasi-protectorate, which meant that American troops could return to the island to protect American interests, lasted from 1901 until 1934. It brought about increased contact and trade between the two countries. To white baseball men like Reds manager and later Washington Senators owner Clark Griffith, Cuba represented a treasure trove of unexploited playing talent. To others, Cuba represented a danger to the baseball color line and American racial values. Cuba, like most Caribbean nations, had a more racially mixed society and a much more liberal attitude toward race than America. Racism American-style made little sense in a country in which members of the same family might range in skin color from dark brown to white—and Jim Crow was unthinkable. Cuban attitudes were very threatening to many white Americans, whose very identity depended on pseudoscientific ideas of racial differences and on the lie that European Americans and African Americans are not related by blood.

The Cuban influence took two forms. One was the new practice of American major league teams traveling to Cuba after the American baseball season for a winter barnstorming tour against local teams. Since it was off-season for African-American clubs, too, Cuban teams were stocked with African-American players who had come down from the United States to earn an extra paycheck. Sometimes these teams held their own or even beat the white major leaguers. Going back to the late 1880s, organized baseball had been uneasy about its teams, particularly championship teams, playing postseason exhibition games against African Americans. In 1887 the (entirely non-Cuban) Cuban Giants had lost to the World Champion Detroit Wolverines by the slim margin of 6–4, after going into the eighth leading 4–2. This was too close for comfort for organized baseball, which first discouraged and later outlawed such games.

A 1909 trip by another Detroit team, the AL champion Tigers, did not help matters. A year after Cuban teams that included African Americans had beaten the Cincinnati Reds in seven games out of 11, the Tigers compiled an equally dismal 4–8 record on their trip to Cuba. One of the Tigers' losses came in the form of a ten-inning no-hitter by Eustaquio Pedroza. Even though they were missing Wahoo Sam Crawford and Ty Cobb, the team's two biggest stars, the Tigers were embarrassed and angry. They returned the following fall, with Crawford, looking for revenge. Their record stood at 3–3–1, including another no-hitter by Pedroza, when they sent for Cobb, who was vacationing in Key West. Cobb, who had just won his fifth batting championship and third stolen-base title, turned the series around, batting .370 and sparking the Tigers to a 4–1 finish. But this time it was Cobb who was angry.

In his first game Cobb was thrown out stealing three times out of three by catcher Bruce Petway; when he tried his famous hook slide into second base, shortstop Pop Lloyd slipped a leg under Cobb and flipped him into the outfield. An avowed racist, Cobb was also embarrassed that he had been shut down by Mendez, the Cuban ace, and outhit by three African Americans. Against the Tigers' big-league pitching, Lloyd hit .500, Grant Johnson hit .412, and Petway hit .390. Cobb publicly vowed never to play against African Americans again. It was a vow that he kept for the rest of his twenty-four-year career in baseball.

American major-league teams played sixty-five games against Cuban teams, nearly all of which included African Americans or Cubans considered too dark-skinned to cross the organized baseball color line. While it is true that not every American team brought along every one of its starting players, half of the teams were pennant winners or World

Champions. Through 1911 the record of American major league teams in Cuba stood at 32 wins, 32 losses, and 1 tie. After the 1911 Athletics went 1–5 on their trip to Cuba, AL President Ban Johnson put an end to all Cuban barnstorming by AL clubs. He made no secret about the reason: "We want no makeshift clubs calling themselves the A's to go to Cuba to be beaten by colored teams." In the 1920s, Baseball Commissioner Kenesaw Mountain Landis extended the ban to both major leagues.

Cubans also influenced organized baseball by coming to play in the United States as individuals. The first to make the trip were outfielder Armando Marsans and third baseman Rafael Almeida, both light-skinned and both signed by Clark Griffith in 1911 to play for the Reds. Many in baseball were alarmed. They felt that this would open the door to Cuban players with more dubious racial backgrounds and undermine the color line. Among African Americans, the arrival of Marsans and Almeida was greeted with great joy and hope for the same reason. As the African-American newspaper the *New York Age* editorialized:

> With the admission of Cubans of a darker hue in the two big leagues, it would then be easy for colored players who are citizens of this country to get into fast company. The Negro in this country has more varied hues than even the Cubans, and the only way to distinguish him would be to hear him talk. Until the public got accustomed to seeing native Negroes on big league teams, the colored players could keep their mouths shut and pass for Cubans.[4]

The "Cuban question" was solved by a compromise. Marsans and Almeida were allowed to stay in organized baseball, but not without going through an insulting charade intended to discourage teams from signing Cubans with the slightest suggestion of African features. In an elaborate public relations gesture, Griffith sent to Cuba for the family histories of the two players going all the way back to Spain. He then announced in the newspapers that he could document that Marsans and Almeida were "two of the purest bars of Castilian soap ever floated to these shores." Other Cubans followed, including pitching great Dolf Luque, who won 194 games in twenty big-league seasons. A pattern developed in which Cuban and other Hispanic players were divided into two groups; the lighter-skinned players were allowed to cross the color line and the darker-skinned players stayed at home or played in the Negro Leagues.

After Luque, Griffith went on to import dozens more Cubans to play for the Senators. All were light-skinned, although many major-league owners continued to fear that the signing of Cubans and other Hispanics would weaken the color line. Since the Cubans, many of the Puerto Ricans, Dominicans, Venezuelans, and other Hispanics who have played in the majors have been subjected to rumors that they are of African descent and passing as white. According to one observer at a major-league owners meeting from the mid-1940s, at which Branch Rickey's plan to break the color line was discussed, Clark Griffith took a firm stand against signing any "niggers." "But, Clark," Rickey reportedly replied, "you already have."

The color line may have withstood the strain caused by the Cuban question, but the forces of racism and Jim Crow were not able to stop all contact between the races, especially away from the major league scene. In spite of the disapproval of the major league baseball establishment, interracial baseball exhibition games and barnstorming matchups continued in various forms, as they had in the 1880s and

1890s. The main reason for this was simple: race sells. As in boxing today, sports fans of the 1900s and 1910s were intrigued by contests that pitted top white clubs against the best African-American competition. Such matches were eagerly attended by fans of both races until the mid-1920s, when Baseball Commissioner Kenesaw Mountain Landis banned all interracial barnstorming by official major league teams. For decades afterward, African-American teams continued to play exhibitions against "all-star" teams made up of white players from different major league clubs. The main reason these games were so hard to stop was because they were so profitable for the players. In 1947, St. Louis Cardinals star Stan Musial complained that his share of the World Series money came to less than half of the $10,000 paycheck he made from one interracial barnstorming tour.

Jim Crow and the color line were also unable to prevent white and African-American baseball players, executives, and owners from having friendships, business dealings, and even teacher-pupil relationships out of the public eye. Starting with the Athletics in 1906 and the Yankees in 1907, major league teams began to rent their ballparks to African-American teams. By the early 1940s, ballpark rentals to Negro League teams had become an important revenue source for major-league clubs. Other business dealings inevitably followed. In addition to his relationship with Anson, Rube Foster was friendly with AL President Ban Johnson and White Sox owner Charlie Comiskey during the 1910s. Athletics owner/manager Connie Mack had ties to the African-American baseball community in Philadelphia. John McGraw hired Rube Foster as a non-uniformed pitching coach; Foster was believed to have taught Hall of Famer Christy Mathewson his famous "fadeaway," or screwball pitch. Rumor also had it that Cubs catcher

Johnny Kling was taught his trademark crouch-and-throw by African-American star Bruce Petway.

By 1920, the racial situation in baseball resembled that in popular music, in which bands, nightclubs, and record companies maintained a strict separation, in public, between African Americans and whites. Offstage, however, it was a different story. For public consumption, the races lived in two separate worlds. Behind the scenes, musicians and ballplayers interacted, learned from each other, and, in many cases, developed great mutual respect.

SECOND-CLASS IMMORTALS

Satchel Paige and the "Black Babe Ruth"

The two big headlines of the 1920 baseball season were Babe Ruth's fifty-four home runs and the breaking of the Black Sox scandal. Ruth smashed the previous single-season home-run record of twenty-nine—which he himself had set the year before—and kicked off the era of modern, home-run-oriented baseball that continues today. Starting in the 1920s, the home run changed from a once-a-week or once-a-month curiosity to the most exciting and most important play in baseball. Hitters gave up trying to slap singles, steal bases, and play hit-and-run and began to imitate the Babe by swinging from the heels on every pitch. Major league home run totals jumped from 447 in 1919 to 631 the following year to 937 the year after that. The trend continued until 1930, when the total number of major league home runs peaked out at over 1,500.

The Black Sox scandal broke when members of the Chicago White Sox shocked the nation by admitting that they had accepted money from gamblers to intentionally lose the 1919 World Series. Eight White

Sox players were tried in a Chicago court for cheating fans who had bet money on the Series. Even though they were acquitted of fraud, the trial left little doubt in anyone's mind that they were morally guilty of not having played to win. Baseball had seen gambling scandals before, but not on this scale. Never before had the sacred institution of the World Series been violated.

Shaken by the Black Sox scandal and terrified that fans would lose their faith in the game's integrity, the major league owners created the office of Commissioner of Baseball to oversee the game and represent the common interests of all of the major league owners. To fill the job they hired a stern, white-haired federal judge named Kenesaw Mountain Landis, who immediately banned the eight Black Sox from baseball for life. The fans seemed satisfied and returned to the ballpark in droves to enjoy the show put on by Ruth and a whole new generation of power-hitters. With the arrival of Commissioner Landis came an era of calm and stability. The turmoil of the turn of the century was forgotten. After the collapse in 1915 of a short-lived rival major league called the Federal League, there was no more labor unrest or infighting over the basic structure of the sport. Organized baseball remained essentially unchanged as America roared through the golden 1920s and limped through the gray depression years of the 1930s.

No commissioner after Landis lasted so long or commanded such respect. Between 1921, when he was appointed, and 1944, when he died in office, he played the part of a benevolent dictator. Landis was a traditionalist, determined to keep baseball on what he saw as the correct moral path. He hated gambling and corruption, and he disciplined dozens of players and owners who became involved with either. Betting on baseball or even being seen at a restaurant with gamblers or organized crime figures would bring down Landis's wrath. He annoyed the owners by waging a long battle to prevent them from dominating the minor leagues and turning them into farm systems. He wanted to preserve the minors as they had always been: independent leagues catering to the fans in their particular towns, cities, and regions. This was one of the few battles he lost.

Landis was more successful in defending traditions that the owners agreed with. One of these was the color line. While he was in office, not only was the color line strictly observed, but he fined or reprimanded anyone in the game who even dared to talk publicly about the subject. Landis was also a smart enough politician to be able to aggressively enforce the owners' Jim Crow policy without having to justify it in public himself. Incredibly, Landis consistently maintained that there was no such thing as the color line. In 1942, after Dodgers manager Leo Durocher was reported as saying that there were "about a million" Negro Leaguers who could play in the majors if it were not for the color line, Landis called him on the carpet of his Chicago office and convinced Durocher that he had been misquoted. "There is no rule," Landis said, "formal or informal, or any understanding—unwritten, subterranean, or sub anything against the hiring of Negro players by the teams of organized baseball."

In the late 1920s and 1930s, however, cracks began to show in baseball's Jim Crow facade. During the Great Depression, ordinary Americans in the North and the South seemed to be gradually losing their stomach for segregation and racial hatred. Sensing this, the forces of white supremacism steeled themselves for a fight. The issues of discrimination and Jim Crow deepened the old divisions between the North and the South. Radical white supremacists stepped up their program of harassment and humiliation of African Americans; the lynchings of the 1910s and 1920s continued. Meanwhile, momentum was building slowly through the 1930s for another civil rights offensive, and an anti-lynching campaign was begun. White novelists and playwrights took up the themes of racial and ethnic injustice; African-American writer Richard Wright won an assortment of literary prizes for his first book, *Uncle Tom's Children*. Labor unions and left-wing politicians agitated against Jim Crow and anti–African-American violence.

Baseball reflected America's racial tension. This was the heyday of the Negro Leagues, a time of such superstars as Smokey Joe Williams, Buck Leonard, Oscar Charleston, Cristobal Torriente, Judy Johnson, Bullet Joe Rogan, Biz Mackey, Martin Dihigo, Cool Papa Bell, Josh Gibson, and Satchel Paige. As it became harder to explain why there was no place in the major leagues—not to mention the minors—for African-American stars of this caliber, organized baseball became increasingly defensive. In 1931, newspaper columnist Westbrook Pegler fired the opening shot in a media attack on the color line that would intensify as the 1930s went on. He ridiculed baseball's racial policies and called the baseball owners hypocrites. "The magnates," he wrote, "haven't the gall to put [the color line] on paper." In 1933, sportswriter Jimmy Powers polled baseball managers and executives on their racial views and discovered that nearly all favored integrating baseball. African-American reporters such as Wendell Smith of the *Pittsburgh Courier*, the country's most prestigious African-American paper, kept up the pressure on the baseball color line. An athlete himself, who had been

Raleigh "Biz" Mackey, a star of the Negro Leagues.

shut out of organized baseball by the color line, Smith's main reason for becoming a journalist was to fight Jim Crow in baseball. In 1945, after Red Sox general manager Eddie Collins said that his team had never considered hiring an African-American player because none had ever asked for a tryout, Smith showed up in Boston with Jackie Robinson and two other Negro Leaguers. The Red Sox were forced to hold the tryout, although it would be fourteen years before the team would sign its first African-American player, Pumpsie Green. In response to criticism from the press, NL President John Heydler repeated the party line that there was no color line. "I do not recall one instance," he said, "where baseball has allowed either race, creed, or color to enter into its selection of players." African Americans, he said, were simply not good enough to play in white baseball. In most major-league cities, however, fans could go to the ballpark when their local major-league team was on the road and see for themselves that this was not true.

There had always been plenty of good African-American players who were unknown outside the small world of African-American baseball. But like a few African-American celebrities in music or show business, some outstanding Negro League stars became so famous they transcended racial boundaries. This had happened in earlier eras. One of the finest African-American ballplayers of the 1910s, shortstop Pop Lloyd, never played a game in organized baseball. But many white fans and most white reporters and players knew who he was. It was the white press that gave Lloyd his nickname of the "Black Honus Wagner." When someone asked Wagner—who was probably the best baseball player in history after Babe Ruth—what he thought about this, he answered that he considered the comparison a compliment. Asked in a radio interview in the 1930s

James "Cool Papa" Bell. The talent of the Negro League
stars eventually made it impossible for organized
baseball to defend the color line.

who he considered the greatest player of all time, Babe Ruth asked, "You mean major leaguers?" "No," the interviewer said, "the greatest player anywhere." "In that case," Ruth answered, "I would pick John Henry Lloyd."

In the same way, Lloyd's contemporaries Oscar Charleston and Spotswood Poles were both called the "Black Ty Cobb." The great Negro League stars of the 1920s and 1930s were also frequently compared with their major league counterparts. Third baseman Judy Johnson was called the "Black Pie Traynor." The title of "Black Babe Ruth," however, was reserved for only one man: Negro League home-run king Josh Gibson. Although accurate statistics were not kept of Negro League seasons and the level of competition that Negro Leaguers faced was variable, Gibson's teammates swore that he hit more home runs in his career than Ruth. If it is also true, as legend has it, that Gibson was the only man ever to hit a fair ball completely out of Yankee Stadium, then perhaps it was Ruth who should have been called the "White Josh Gibson."

JOSH GIBSON

Joshua "Josh" Gibson was born in 1911 in a small town in Georgia. When he was twelve, Gibson's father moved the family to Pittsburgh, Pennsylvania, a hotbed of African-American baseball. Already over six feet tall and incredibly muscular at eighteen, Josh Gibson broke in as a catcher in 1930 with the local Negro League team, the Homestead Grays. He spent most of the next dozen years playing for the Grays and another Pittsburgh team, the Crawfords.

Wherever he went, Gibson hit home runs. Like Babe Ruth, he hit them long and he hit them often. Also like Ruth, Gibson hit for average; he was credited

Many consider William Julius "Judy" Johnson to have been the best third baseman in any league in the 1920s.

with batting averages of .393 in 1942 and .380 in 1932. Because of the lack of reliable statistics, Negro League history is a mixture of fact, fiction, and folk-tales. By some accounts, Gibson hit seventy-nine home runs in one season, eighty-five in another. He was reported to have hit home runs that were 500, 550, even 580 feet long. (The longest Babe Ruth home run has been estimated at around 550 feet.) One day in Yankee Stadium, Gibson launched a massive shot that some witnesses claim left the park on the fly. Others who were there say that the ball hit the top of the outer stadium fence. Either way, this was probably the longest home run ever hit in the home park of Ruth and Gehrig.

Whatever the exact numbers, people who saw Josh Gibson and players who played with him considered him a good defensive catcher and the greatest power hitter they had ever seen. Monte Irvin, who played in the Negro Leagues, Winter Leagues, and the major leagues with the New York Giants, has called Gibson "without a doubt, the greatest hitter I ever saw, black or white." If Gibson had been allowed to cross the color line, according to Irvin, "He would have broken Ruth's record." In the 1930s, white Hall of Fame pitcher Walter Johnson gave his opinion of Gibson: "There is a catcher that any big-league club would like to buy for $200,000. . . . He hits the ball a mile. And he catches so easy he might as well be in a rocking chair. Throws like a rifle. Bill Dickey isn't as good a catcher. Too bad this Gibson is a colored fellow."

By his sheer skill, Josh Gibson was a walking (or trotting) argument against the baseball color line. Like Bud Fowler, Frank Grant, and the other African-American stars of the 1880s, players like Gibson sorely tempted individual major league owners to sign them for their teams in spite of the color line. The temptation was especially great for owners of losing teams. In 1939, president Bill Benswanger of the sixth-place Pittsburgh Pirates defied Landis by inviting Gibson for a tryout. He later backed off. In 1942, tired of watching Gibson's tape-measure shots and seeing the Grays outdraw his seventh-place Senators in their own ballpark, Washington owner Clark Griffith met with Gibson and teammate Buck Leonard. Griffith, of course, was the man who had raised the Cuban question by signing Marsans and Almeida in 1911. "He talked to us about Negro baseball and about the trouble there would be if he took us into the big leagues," Leonard later recalled, "but he never made us an offer."

Soon after this conversation, Josh Gibson retired from baseball at thirty-four, suffering from blackouts and severe headaches. He died of a stroke in 1947, just three months before Jackie Robinson's debut with the Brooklyn Dodgers. Gibson was elected to the Baseball Hall of Fame in 1972.

Few contemporary major-league players denied the skill of Gibson and his fellow Negro League stars, at least in private. They knew how good they were from personal experience. As in the 1900s and 1910s, many major leaguers played in exhibition games against African Americans or played integrated winter base ball with them in Cuba, Puerto Rico, Mexico, the Dominican Republic, Panama, or Venezuela. Because of Landis's edict, there were no more interracial games involving intact major league teams, and white players were forbidden to wear their major league uniforms in such games. Instead, the interracial contests of the 1920s and 1930s took the form of "all-star" teams made up of white players from different major league teams, sometimes supplemented by minor leaguers, going against similarly mixed African-

American squads or whole Negro League teams. Sometimes, a white team and an African-American team would join up for a barnstorming tour and play a series of games in different cities around the country. In the most famous of these tours, one led by St. Louis Cardinals pitcher Dizzy Dean and another by Cleveland Indians pitcher Bob Feller, the African-American teams more than held their own against big-league opposition. The thousands of white fans who attended these games saw how good Negro League baseball really was. The tours made a national celebrity out of Satchel Paige, who by the mid-1930s was a household name with fans of both races. According to an accounting by historian John Holway, out of the 400 interracial exhibition games played before 1948 that involved major leaguers, the African-American teams won 268.

The African-American players themselves had no doubt that they were as good as most major leaguers. As Negro Leaguer Gene Benson said, "We always played the major leaguers and we knew that there wasn't any difference because we used to always beat them after the season was over." Many whites agreed. "It's too bad those colored boys don't play in the big league," Dizzy Dean said, "because they sure got some great players." Detroit Tigers catcher Birdie Tebbetts admitted that "we were all in awe of Satchel Paige."

Babe Ruth's Yankee teammate Lou Gehrig risked Commissioner Landis's wrath by stating: "I have seen many Negro players who should be in the major leagues. There is no room in baseball for discrimination. It is our national pastime and a game for all." Chicago Cubs manager Gabby Hartnett joined fellow managers Jimmy Dykes and Leo Durocher in being slapped on the wrist for publicly lusting after African-American talent. "If managers were given permission," Hartnett said in a 1940 interview, "there'd be a mad rush to sign up Negroes."

SATCHEL PAIGE

It is likely that Leroy "Satchel" Paige won more professional baseball games than any other pitcher in history. Cy Young, of course, is the all-time major league leader, with 511 wins. But he played in organized baseball, in which the season never lasted more than 150 games or so, pitched in a regular rotation with other pitchers, and rarely participated in exhibition games. From 1926 to 1947 Paige pitched for Negro League teams that sometimes played 200 or more games a year. He was in such demand as a gate attraction that he often pitched several games in a row or was "lent" to another team between starts.

Each spring he pitched down South. Each fall he barnstormed against African-American clubs and white "all-star" teams. After that, Paige headed South to star in the Winter leagues of the Dominican Republic, Venezuela, and Mexico. Paige himself claimed in 1961 that he had won over 2,000 games.

No one is sure exactly what year Paige was born, but he pitched as a rookie in the major leagues for the Cleveland Indians in 1948, when he was somewhere between the ages of forty-two and fifty. The *Sporting News* ripped Indians owner Bill Veeck for signing a player as old as Paige, calling it a demeaning publicity stunt, but Paige went 6–1 with a 2.47 ERA and helped the Indians to the AL pennant. It was also an effective publicity stunt: Satchel Paige was on the mound the night Cleveland set the all-time night-game attendance record of 78,382. When he recorded his last major-league pitching decision with the St. Louis Browns in 1953, Paige may have been in his middle to late fifties. He continued to pitch in exhibitions through the mid-1960s.

The lanky, young Satchel Paige was a Negro League legend because of his blazing fastball, pin-

In the 1930s and 1940s, Negro League pitcher Satchel Paige was better known—and better paid— than most major league players.

point control and amazing charisma. Tall tales seemed to spring up wherever Paige went. Supposedly, several times he called his outfielders into the infield and struck out the opposing side. According to other stories, Paige liked to show off by telling the batter what pitch was coming; in one game he wrote "FAST-BALL" in big letters on the bottom of his left shoe. He demonstrated his control by pitching strike after strike, using a handkerchief for home plate, or by pitching balls between two bats standing on home plate six inches apart. His stamina was legendary, too, until he badly injured his arm in 1938. After that Paige learned to get batters out with control and a famous assortment of change-ups and breaking pitches. These included his "bat dodger," the "two-hump blooper," and the "hesitation pitch," in which Paige would distract the batter by pausing in mid-windup.

Paige never lost his magnetic personality and star appeal. Former teammate Jimmy Crutchfield said, "When Satchel got to that ballpark, it was like the sun just came out." Fans flocked to see him and Paige was paid accordingly. In 1942, when he earned $37,000—more than four times the average major leaguer's salary—Paige announced that the majors "couldn't pay me enough to join." During the war years, he was probably the highest-paid baseball player in the country, African American or white. The exhibition tours of Dean, Feller, Ruth, Gomez, and others added to the Satchel Paige mystique. In 1935 the Yankees sent a scout to the West Coast to observe Joe DiMaggio, then a young minor-leaguer, play against an African-American team that included Satchel Paige. The scout telegraphed back: "DiMaggio all we hoped he'd be. Hit Satch one for four."

When the Dodgers signed Jackie Robinson in 1947, Paige was disappointed that he was not the one. As he later wrote in his autobiography, *Maybe*

Legendary former Negro League third baseman and longtime major league scout Judy Johnson is welcomed into the Hall of Fame by Baseball Commissioner Bowie Kuhn.

I'll Pitch Forever, "I'd been the guy who started all that big talk about letting us in the big time. . . . It was still me that ought to have been first." But he publicly rooted for Jackie Robinson and never became bitter or lost his dry sense of humor. When it decided to accept Negro Leaguers in the early 1970s, the Baseball Hall of Fame originally planned to honor them in a separate part of the building from the white major leaguers. Many outraged fans and sportswriters protested that this separation smacked of Jim Crow, and shortly before Satchel Paige's induction ceremony the Hall of Fame changed its mind. In his acceptance speech, however, Paige could not resist tweaking baseball over the controversy. He solemnly thanked the Hall for turning him from a "second-class citizen" into a "second-class immortal."

The heat on organized baseball to end the color line reached the boiling point in the late 1930s. The timing was influenced in part by international politics. By the mid-1930s, it was becoming more and more obvious that the rise of Adolf Hitler and the racist Nazi party in Germany was a potential threat to the United States. The 1936 Olympics, held in Germany, were used by the Nazis to promote their ideas of the racial superiority of Germanic peoples to Jews, Africans, and other groups. Most Americans were repelled by Nazism and overjoyed when African-American sprinter Jesse Owens embarrassed the Germans by winning several gold medals. Besides making an African-American athlete a national hero in the United States, the Nazis and their vile racist and anti-Semitic politics also discredited white supremacism back in the United States.

When the war came, and American soldiers of both races were fighting and dying to defeat the Nazis, racial segregation (including in the armed forces) began to look even more indefensible to white

America. The Jim Crow policy in baseball—an institution that asked for exemptions from wartime restrictions based on its status as a patriotic institution—seemed particularly obscene.

Jim Crow also became an issue in the propaganda war between capitalism and communism. American communists took up the cause of the baseball color line. During World War II, communists picketed outside major-league ballparks; one African-American picketer carried a sign that read: IF WE CAN STOP BULLETS, WHY NOT BALLS? In 1942 Nat Lowe, sports editor of the communist *Daily Worker,* embarrassed the baseball owners by bringing Negro League stars such as Roy Campanella to major league parks for tryouts. The Russian communists scored points in many parts of the world by using the KKK, racial segregation, and the lynchings of African Americans to discredit American capitalism and democracy. In 1952 the United States Attorney-general gave a speech in which he criticized racial discrimination in America because it provided "grist for the communist propaganda mills."

The Jake Powell incident of 1938 also put the spotlight on baseball and race. A backup outfielder and pinch-hitter for the Yankees, Powell was the type who, in the phrase of one African-American leader, "causes race riots." An unpleasant character with a history of on-field fighting, Powell once broke Detroit Tigers outfielder Hank Greenberg's wrist in a scuffle that had anti-Semitic overtones. During the pregame show on a Chicago radio station before a White Sox–Yankees game, announcer Bob Elson asked Powell how he spent the off-season. Powell answered that he worked as a policeman in Dayton, Ohio, where he kept in shape by "cracking niggers over the head." Elson immediately cut off the interview, but the station was inundated with angry phone calls.

Most of the white press tried to pass off Powell's remark as a lame joke by an unsophisticated Southerner. Actually, Powell was born in Maryland and lived in Ohio. Meanwhile, African-American leaders organized protests and threatened to boycott a beer company belonging to Jake Ruppert, the owner of the Yankees, unless Powell was punished. Whether it was for the sake of Ruppert's beer business or for public relations reasons, Commissioner Landis suspended Powell for ten days. The Yankees arranged for Powell to go to Harlem in New York City to apologize to the African-American community in person.

Westbrook Pegler and other liberal newspaper columnists took the Powell incident and beat organized baseball over the head with it. Baseball "trades under the name of the national game," Pegler wrote, "but has always treated the Negroes as Adolf Hitler treats the Jews." New York *Daily News* writer Lloyd Lewis argued that Powell's punishment was too lenient, "especially in a time when America is looming up, more and more every day, as the one place where racial prejudice is unfashionable." On the first day back from his suspension, Powell was greeted with a shower of pop bottles thrown by African-American fans. Powell played only a few dozen more games with the Yankees before being traded to the Senators. He retired in 1945, and in 1948, committed suicide while under arrest in a Washington, D.C., police station on a charge of passing bad checks.

By the late 1930s all these incidents indicated to many in baseball that integration was on the way. In 1938 Clark Griffith said that the end of segregation was "not far off." Even NL president Ford Frick said that "baseball is biding its time and waiting for the social change which is inevitable. Times are changing." An added factor was the terrible shortage of playing talent caused by the military draft. Since

Satchel Paige (left) and Bill Veeck.

fewer African Americans were drafted, the problem
was not nearly so severe in the Negro Leagues.
Desperate for players, the St. Louis Browns recruited
washed-up minor league pitcher Sig Jackucki from
a Texas industrial league—and won the pennant. In
1943 the Cardinals, who had lost 265 players from
their farm system to the draft, actually advertised
for players in the "Help Wanted" section of the
Sporting News. Of course, nothing stood between the
major league clubs and the plentiful, veteran talent of

the Negro Leagues except the weakening color line that baseball insisted did not exist.

But the color line was not dead yet. It would be more than eight long years after the Jake Powell incident before an African American would play in the major leagues. In 1943 maverick minor-league owner Bill Veeck came up with a daring plan to integrate baseball. As with most Veeck ideas, this one was guaranteed to provoke maximum public controversy. His plan was to buy the also-ran Philadelphia Phillies, stock the team with the best players he could find in the Negro Leagues and start winning. "I had not the slightest doubt," Veeck later wrote, "that in 1944, a war year, the Phils would have leaped from seventh-place to the pennant." He reached a handshake agreement to buy the club but made the fatal mistake of traveling to Chicago to give Commissioner Landis advance notice of what he intended to do. According to Veeck, Landis gave no indication at their meeting that he opposed the plan, but Veeck awoke the next morning to find that Landis had hoodwinked him. The Phillies had been taken over by the National League.

The team was then sold to a man named William Cox for half of what Veeck would have paid. Cox was later banned from baseball by Landis for betting on his own team.

When the story of Jackie Robinson and the integration of baseball is told, it is often said that baseball was ahead of its time. For instance, the Supreme Court decision in the case of *Brown* v. *the Board of Education of Topeka, Kansas,* which overturned the "separate but equal" doctrine and held that segregation in public schools was unconstitutional, did not come until 1954. Countless institutions, clubs, and professions did not integrate until much later than 1954; some remain all-white today. While this is certainly true, when you consider the tremendous pressure on baseball in the late 1930s and early 1940s to break the color line, it may be more to the point to ask: what took baseball so long? In his autobiography, former NL president and baseball commissioner Ford Frick gives his answer:

> *What baseball operators had done through the years was bow abjectly to what they thought was overwhelming public opinion. They were afraid to make a move. They were afraid of upsetting the status quo, afraid of alienating the white clientele that largely supported the professional game.*[1]

This explanation is too kind to the owners. The baseball owners may have tried to pass the responsibility to the players or the fans, but the facts suggest that they enforced the color line in the 1930s and early 1940s for the same reason they drew the color line in the 1880s—because they believed in it. Opposition from fans or players does not explain why some major league owners refused to hire a single African-American player for ten or even twelve years after the Dodgers, Indians, and other teams were integrated. Like a stodgy old men's club, organized baseball was slow to change because discrimination and exclusion were part of its identity.

THE BADGE OF MARTYRDOM

The Myth of Rickey and Robinson

The United States entered World War II shortly after the Japanese attacked Pearl Harbor, in December 1941. Congress declared war on Nazi Germany as well and American troops began to fight in two theaters: in Asia against the Japanese and in Europe and North Africa against the Germans. Millions of Americans enlisted or were drafted into the armed forces. This caused a severe labor shortage in many American industries. Just as it had during World War I, this labor shortage forced American industry to open up to women and African Americans jobs that had been previously held only by white men. President Roosevelt pushed the process along by establishing the Federal Commission on Fair Employment Practices to combat racial discrimination.

Many African Americans moved into better jobs because of the war. A big difference between World War I and World War II was that the positive gains made in World War II by African Americans continued after the cease-fire. There was no repeat of the riots of 1919. African Americans and the government continued the push for racial reforms. In 1942 New York

State passed the Quinn-Ives Act, prohibiting racial discrimination in hiring; in 1945 it established the New York State Commission Against Discrimination, the first state agency of its kind in the country. In 1946 President Harry S. Truman set up federal commissions on higher education and civil rights to try to remedy segregation and racial discrimination in those areas. That same year, the navy began to experiment with racially mixed units; in 1948 Truman ordered the army to desegregate. Voters began to send politicians to Washington who spoke out against racism and segregation. Around this time, Minnesota elected Hubert Humphrey, who became the first consistent congressional voice in favor of civil rights for African Americans.

Baseball experienced a wartime labor shortage, too. Led by Hank Greenberg and Bob Feller, hundreds of major leaguers and minor leaguers left their teams and went off to war. President Franklin D. Roosevelt allowed baseball to continue as an aid to morale on the home front. But by 1943 enough of the top players had enlisted or been drafted that the quality of play in the majors suffered greatly. Still, the major league owners refused to hire African Americans from the Negro Leagues. Even after the death of Commissioner Landis in 1944, organized baseball held fast to the color line. The new commissioner, Senator Happy Chandler of Kentucky, gave African Americans hope by telling the *Pittsburgh Courier*: "If [African Americans] can fight and die on Okinawa, Guadalcanal, in the South Pacific, they can play ball in America." But nothing changed. In 1946 the sixteen major league owners met in secret to vote on the question of whether to allow African Americans into the majors. The result of the vote was 15–1 against. Branch Rickey, representing the Brooklyn Dodgers, cast the only vote in favor.

Rickey voted yes because he had already decided to promote former Negro League shortstop Jackie Robinson to Brooklyn in 1947. Rickey had signed Robinson to a minor league contract before the 1946 season and sent him to the Dodger farm system. The team he chose was the Dodgers' top minor-league club, the Montreal Royals of the International League—the same International League in which Bud Fowler, George Stovey, Fleet Walker, and Frank Grant had played in the 1880s. On April 18, 1946— opening day—Robinson stepped up to the plate wearing the blue and white Montreal uniform. The baseball color line was broken. Robinson went four for five with two stolen bases as the Royals destroyed the Jersey City Giants, 14–1. As Branch Rickey told the story years later, this was the culmination of years of careful planning and waiting for the right moment to break the baseball color line.

BRANCH RICKEY

Wesley Branch Rickey was born in 1881 into a strict Methodist family in Southeastern Ohio. When he became a professional baseball player, after briefly coaching a college baseball team, he promised his mother that he would never play on Sundays. This promise and an arm injury limited his major league career to 119 games with the Browns and the Yankees.

After earning a law degree at the University of Michigan, Rickey returned to baseball as the manager of the Browns. In 1919 he moved across town to serve as president and manager of the Cardinals. It soon became clear that Rickey's talents lay in scouting and player development rather than on-field managing. Cardinals owner Sam Breadon hired Rogers Hornsby to manage the team and kicked Rickey upstairs. A genius at recognizing and judging base-ball talent, Rickey turned the Cardinals into one of the great National League dynasties. On the principle that "quality comes out of quantity," he invented the first farm system. Rickey got financial control of thir-ty-two minor league teams, containing over six hun-dred players, and turned them into schools for baseball. Rickey hired the best instructors, scouts, and coaches and pioneered the use of batting cages, pitching machines, batting helmets and efficient prac-tice drills. For the next twenty-five years, this sys-tem provided a steady stream of talent that won the Cardinals eight pennants. Strangely, the churchgo-ing, teetotaling Rickey seemed drawn to physically aggressive, hard-partying ballplayers, such as Leo Durocher and Pepper Martin of the colorful "Gas House Gang" team of 1934. Other stars of the 1934 Cardinals were Dizzy Dean, Frankie Frisch, and Joe Medwick. Rickey's farm system also provided plenty of players to trade and sell to other teams for cash. At one time there were sixty-five St. Louis products playing in the eight-team National League.

After a falling-out with Breadon, Rickey moved to Brooklyn to run the Dodgers. According to Rickey, he began almost immediately to plan a way to break the baseball color line. Rickey told the story of a racial incident that occurred during his early college coach-ing days at Ohio Wesleyan that left a lasting mark on him. In 1904 the team traveled to South Bend, Indiana, to play Notre Dame. One of Rickey's play-ers was an African American named Charley Thomas. When they arrived at their hotel, however, they were told that African Americans were not welcome. By threatening to move the team elsewhere, Rickey con-vinced the hotel to allow Thomas to stay on a cot in Rickey's room, as if he were a servant. When Rickey went to his room later that night, Thomas was sitting on the edge of the bed in tears, rubbing his hands. "It's my skin, Mr. Rickey," he cried. "If I could just make it go away I'd be like everybody else." Rickey claimed that he never forgot that scene and spent most of his sixty years in baseball waiting for the chance to do something about racism.

Rickey saw that chance when he was hired as president of the Brooklyn Dodgers. According to Arthur Mann, Rickey's friend and biographer, while reporting to the Dodgers board of directors on his plan to set up a mass scouting system, Rickey mentioned that he "might include a Negro player or two." That was in 1942, his first year with the Dodgers. Three years later Rickey announced that he intended to establish a new Negro league called the United States League. The plan called for a Brooklyn franchise named the Brooklyn Brown Dodgers that would play in the Dodgers ballpark, Ebbets Field. Someday, Rickey said, the United States League might be merged into organized baseball. But the United States League never got off the ground and the Brown Dodgers folded after only one year. Rickey later revealed that the whole thing had been a smokescreen. Its real purpose, he said, was to provide a cover so that Rickey could send his scouts to find an African-American player to break the color line without arousing the suspicion of the other baseball owners.

In Rickey's mind, that player had to be a special kind of person. Mindful of the abuse that Fowler, Grant, and the others had taken from fans and fellow players in the International League in the 1880s, Rickey feared that if the first African American across the color line was too sensitive or had too short a temper, the result would be ugly racial confrontations on the field or in the stands. This would give racist owners the perfect excuse for redrawing the color line.

"I had to get a man," Rickey said, "who would carry the badge of martyrdom. The press had to accept him. He had to stimulate a good reaction to the Negro race itself for an unfortunate one might have solidified the antagonism of other colors. And I had to consider the man's teammates."

Rickey meant that the player had to be acceptable to whites. In 1944 and 1945 Rickey had superscout Clyde Sukeforth and others out looking for the right man. In August 1945 Rickey told Sukeforth to concentrate his efforts on Jackie Robinson. Robinson had two things going for him: he was well educated and he was comfortable in white society. Robinson had attended the University of California at Los Angeles and he had starred on the school's integrated football team. If Sukeforth liked Robinson's potential as a baseball player, he was to bring him to Brooklyn for a meeting with Rickey. When Sukeforth caught up with Robinson's team, the Kansas City Monarchs, Robinson was injured and could not play. But Sukeforth was very impressed with Robinson's personality. "There was something about that man that just gripped you," Sukeforth later remembered, "He was tough, he was intelligent, and he was proud." Although Robinson was skeptical and quizzed Sukeforth about Rickey's purposes, he agreed to the meeting.

Alone with Robinson in the Dodgers downtown Brooklyn offices, Rickey explained that he wanted to break the baseball color line by signing Robinson to a Montreal contract. He delivered a passionate sermon on the hostility, beanballs, and spikings that Robinson would face and why he had to accept them without

*Jackie Robinson in 1946, wearing the uniform
of the International League Montreal Royals.*

retaliation. "You will symbolize a crucial cause," Rickey said. "One incident, just one incident, can set it back twenty years." Even though he was so personally prudish that he never uttered a stronger curse than "Judas Priest," Rickey vividly acted out the vile insults Robinson would have to endure: "dirty black son of a bitch, nigger bastard, coon!" Robinson later said that the performance was so convincing that he nearly jumped up and took a swing at Rickey. "Are you looking for a man who is afraid to fight back?," Robinson asked. "No," said Rickey, "I'm looking for a ballplayer with guts enough not to fight back." After thinking for a few minutes, Jackie Robinson promised to try to turn the other cheek.

Robinson's signing was met with furious protests by other baseball owners, but other than passing a resolution condemning the move at their 1946 owners meeting, no real action was taken. As Robinson rolled along in Montreal on his way to the IL batting title at .349, a strange passivity descended over baseball. The Dodgers signed four more African-American players, including catcher Roy Campanella and pitcher Don Newcombe, but no other team followed suit. Commissioner Happy Chandler had nothing to say about the signings. The rest of organized baseball seemed to be waiting to see what Rickey was going to do next. One likely reason for this was fear of public opinion, which was increasingly opposed to segregation; another was fear of prosecution under the new civil rights laws. As far as the law was concerned, keeping a secret "gentleman's agreement" was one thing—openly taking a player's job away because of race was another.

During the winter of 1946–47, Rickey prepared for Robinson's arrival in the major leagues. He met quietly with clergy and other leaders of the African-American community in Brooklyn to ask their help in toning down the enthusiasm of African-American fans. Afraid of a white backlash, Rickey urged them not to hurt Robinson's chances as African-American fans in Chicago supposedly had spoiled Charlie "Chief Tokohama" Grant's in 1901.

When the white backlash came, however, it was not from the fans but from Rickey's own players. During spring training of 1947, several of Robinson's teammates signed a petition stating that they would refuse to play with an African American. When he heard about this, Dodgers manager Leo Durocher hauled the petitioners out of bed in the middle of the night and told them what they could do with the petition. He then gave a short lecture on his racial philosophy: "I don't care if the guy is yellow or black or has stripes like a ——ing zebra. I'm the manager of this team and I say he plays. What's more, I say he can make us all rich." Rickey offered to trade any of the group who wanted out. The matter was dropped. No copies of the petition survive and different players have different memories of who was involved, but the names that come up in most accounts are Dixie Walker, Carl Furillo, Bobby Bragan, and Eddie Stanky. Many journalists and historians describe the group as completely or almost completely made up of Southerners, but this is not true. Bragan and Walker were from the South. Eddie Stanky lived in the South but had grown up and gone to high school in Philadelphia. Furillo was also from Pennsylvania. And a pair of Southerners, Pee Wee Reese and Kirby Higbe, helped to foil the petition. Respected team leader Reese pointedly refused to sign it and Higbe was the one who informed on the petitioners to Durocher.

Robinson was not given much of a chance by many reporters and players around the National League. Bob Feller said that Robinson was muscle-bound and had no future in baseball. Even some Negro Leaguers were publicly skeptical that Robinson could make it.

Anonymous hate letters and death threats arrived in Robinson's mailbox by the dozens. Under incredible psychological pressure, Jackie Robinson hit .297 for the Dodgers in 1947 and led the NL in stolen bases, with twenty-nine.

Robinson did not find the National League to be a very friendly place. In Philadelphia, the Dodgers' team hotel refused to give him a room. In the early part of the season, the attitude of his teammates toward him ranged from lukewarm to hostile. During a card game, Dodgers pitcher Hugh Casey humiliated Robinson by rubbing his head "for good luck" in front of several teammates. Just as Rickey had predicted, opposing teams subjected him to a torrent of awful verbal abuse and spikings, and pitchers aimed at his head. Robinson was hit by pitches nine times in 1947. Rickey had counted on this to rally the rest of the Dodgers to Robinson's side. One day in Philadelphia, it happened. Led by manager Ben Chapman, a man who in his playing days was run out of New York for making anti-Semitic remarks, the Phillies were treating Robinson to a barrage of especially vile insults. Knowing about the death threats, Phillies players pointed bats at him from the bench and made machine-gun noises. Finally Eddie Stanky had enough and challenged the Phillies bench. "Why don't you guys go to work on somebody who can fight back?" Stanky yelled. "There isn't one of you has the guts of a louse." Dodgers team leader and shortstop Pee Wee Reese also stuck up for Robinson, and later the two became close friends. When the 1947 season was over, Jackie Robinson took home the NL Rookie of the Year award—and an ulcer.

Rickey's plan had succeeded and there was no turning back. Bill Veeck signed outfielder Larry Doby for the Cleveland Indians and soon Negro League stars began to cross the color line in a slow but steady

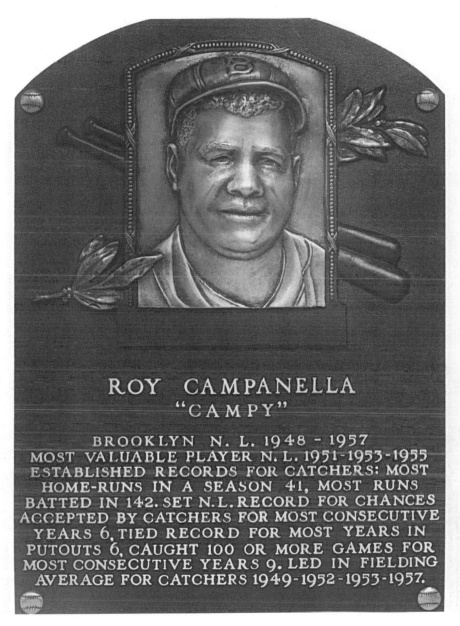

ROY CAMPANELLA
"CAMPY"

BROOKLYN N. L. 1948 - 1957
MOST VALUABLE PLAYER N. L. 1951-1953-1955
ESTABLISHED RECORDS FOR CATCHERS: MOST
HOME-RUNS IN A SEASON 41, MOST RUNS
BATTED IN 142. SET N.L. RECORD FOR CHANCES
ACCEPTED BY CATCHERS FOR MOST CONSECUTIVE
YEARS 6, TIED RECORD FOR MOST YEARS IN
PUTOUTS 6, CAUGHT 100 OR MORE GAMES FOR
MOST CONSECUTIVE YEARS 9. LED IN FIELDING
AVERAGE FOR CATCHERS 1949-1952-1953-1957.

*Roy Campanella's Baseball Hall
of Fame plaque.*

stream. Willard Brown, Hank Thompson, and Dan Bankhead entered the majors in late 1947. In 1948 they were joined by Roy Campanella and Satchel Paige.

In 1950 Branch Rickey was forced out by new Dodgers owner Walter O'Malley. Rickey went to Pittsburgh, where he rebuilt the Pirates farm system, stole Roberto Clemente from the Dodgers, and laid the foundation for the team's rebirth in the late 1950s. In 1959 he forced organized baseball to expand by threatening to form a third major league, called the Continental League. The New York Mets and the Houston Astros came out of Rickey's efforts. In 1967, he was elected to the Hall of Fame, at least in part for his role in the breaking of the color line.

Branch Rickey's version of how he and Jackie Robinson broke the baseball color line has gone down in history as the whole truth. But there is reason to be skeptical about some parts of Rickey's story, in particular his motives. One reason for this is that at some point in the mid-1940s everyone in baseball, including Rickey, realized that integration was coming and that history would not be kind to those who opposed it. Nobody wanted to be remembered as a racist. In the aftermath of Jackie Robinson's breaking of the color line, many key baseball figures scrambled to rewrite the stories of their own roles in the affair—usually casting themselves as the heroes. Pirates president Bill Benswanger, for instance, claimed that in the 1930s he had tried "more than once" to sign Josh Gibson but that Homestead Grays' owner Cum Posey had stopped him. Wendell Smith called this "unmitigated story-telling." NL president and later commissioner Ford Frick, who in 1943 helped Landis sabotage Bill Veeck's attempt to integrate the Phillies, leaked a newspaper story in 1947 that he had headed off a strike by racist St. Louis Cardinals players who did not want to play against Jackie Robinson by threatening them with long suspensions. "I don't care if the whole league strikes," Frick was quoted as saying. "Those who do it will encounter quick retribution." The only problem with this story is that it probably is not true. None of the Cardinals has ever backed up the story; Wendell Smith doubted that it happened at all.

The president of the self-nominated hero society was Commissioner Happy Chandler. Chandler spent much of his later life campaigning for some of the credit for breaking the baseball color line. He claimed that he and Rickey were secretly working together all along and that Rickey even asked him for permission to go ahead with the signing of Robinson. "I have never understood," said Chandler years later, "why Branch Rickey took the full credit for breaking the color line with Jackie Robinson. If I hadn't approved the contract transfer from Montreal, the Dodgers farm team, to Brooklyn, Robinson couldn't have played. No chance." If Chandler had not approved Robinson's contract transfer from Montreal, he probably would have opened up organized baseball to a devastating lawsuit or civil rights prosecution. Other than Chandler's own word, there is no evidence that Chandler took any action against the color line or gave Rickey or Robinson any help at all.

As for Rickey's motives, while he himself did not deny that his primary purpose in breaking the color line was to sign winning ballplayers, Rickey did claim to oppose segregation on moral grounds. There was the Charley Thomas incident, during the time Rickey was coaching at Ohio Wesleyan. As he explained, "I couldn't face my God much longer knowing that His black creatures are held separate from His white creatures in the game that has given me all I own." The problem with that is that Rickey was sixty-five in 1946; he had spent forty-two years in professional baseball. At no other time had he made any protest over organized baseball's Jim Crow policies. During the two decades that Rickey ran the St. Louis Cardinals, the Cardinals were the only team in the majors to have segregated stands. In the park in which Rickey's team played, "black creatures" could not sit in the grandstand with "white creatures." Even the St. Louis press box was segregated. Years later, Rickey claimed that he had tried to desegregate the stands, but it is hard to understand what would have stopped him. The Cardinals owner, New Yorker Sam Breadon, was one of the more liberal owners regarding race, and no city or state law required white and African-American fans and reporters to be separated at the St. Louis ballpark. There is no independent evidence that Rickey ever attempted to do anything about either situation.

Bill Veeck and others have also doubted that Branch Rickey's original purpose in scouting Negro League ballplayers was really, as he claimed, to find the right man to break the color line. Is it possible that in the beginning, Rickey was serious about starting a new Negro League called the United States League and that he was scouting Negro League players to sign them for the Brown Dodgers? For one thing, Rickey never told Clyde Sukeforth, described by historian Donald Honig as "one of Rickey's most trusted lieutenants," that he was really scouting players for the Dodgers. He also instructed Sukeforth to hide his presence from the Negro League teams. "Mr. Rickey told us," Sukeforth later said, "he didn't want this idea of his getting around, about the Brooklyn Brown Dodgers; that nobody was supposed to know what we were doing." When he scouted Negro League games, Sukeforth was to sit in the stands as if he were an ordinary fan and not let on why he was there. This makes a lot of sense if Rickey was plotting to rob the Negro Leagues of large numbers of their players and form a competing league. The reason for this secrecy, however, is not so clear if the Brown Dodgers were just a cover story. Why keep a cover story a secret? Furthermore, when Rickey met with Campanella and Newcombe in October of 1945—after he had already signed Robinson—and offered them contracts, both players came away with the impression that Rickey had been trying to sign them for the Brown Dodgers, not the white club. It is hard to imagine how Newcombe, who actually signed a contract, could have been mistaken about what team he was agreeing to join.

One explanation for all this could be that Rickey was moving cautiously toward breaking the color line in the early to mid-1940s but that he was not sure if or when it would be possible. If the experiment of putting Jackie Robinson in Montreal failed, then he had a backup plan. The backup plan was to go ahead with the United States League and the Brown Dodgers. By setting up a new, white-owned Negro League, Rickey would very likely damage or destroy the existing Negro Leagues, but he would gain control of a vast pool of baseball talent. When integration did come to baseball, Rickey would have his pick of African-American players for the Dodgers. Rickey certainly felt no sympathy for the Negro Leagues, which he described as a "racket" run by gangsters. During the late 1940s, when a few major league clubs were signing Negro League players left and right, AL owner Bill Veeck always paid the Negro League teams compensation for their players. Rickey consistently refused to pay a dime.

Like any good politician, Branch Rickey was a master at appearing to lead events that were actually leading him. Rickey spent his entire professional life trying to amass as much baseball talent as possible. All that untapped Negro League talent must have tempted Branch Rickey more than anyone in organized baseball, especially during the war years, when white players were so scarce. It would certainly be in character for him to have tried to get his hands on that talent any way he could and work out later how best to exploit it.

Why did Rickey sign Jackie Robinson? Part of his motivation may have been the Charley Thomas incident and a genuine desire to do the right thing. It is more likely, however, that Rickey's prime motivation was that he believed Jackie Robinson could help the Dodgers win—and that in the racial climate of 1947 he thought he could get away with signing him. The bottom line is that Rickey was the one who, in the short term, benefited the most from the breaking of the color line. Jackie Robinson was able to play in the major leagues, but at great personal cost. African Americans in general gained a few major league jobs, but they lost the Negro Leagues, one of the country's largest African American–owned businesses. The Negro Leagues went broke almost immediately after 1947. As soon as African-American fans realized that integration had come to organized baseball to stay, they abandoned the Negro Leagues and flocked to major and minor league parks to see their favorites play on white teams. The hundreds of ex–Negro Leaguers who did not get jobs with white clubs were left unemployed. But Branch Rickey and the Brooklyn Dodgers got Jackie Robinson, Dan Bankhead, Roy Campanella, Don Newcombe, Sandy Amoros, Joe Black, and Junior Gilliam. For all of this talent, they paid exactly nothing. Between 1947 and 1956 the Dodgers won seven pennants and one World Series.

JACKIE ROBINSON

The real hero of the breaking of the baseball color line is Jackie Robinson. The grandson of a slave, Robinson was born in Georgia in 1919, the year of the Chicago race riot and the Red Summer. The family moved to southern California when he was young. A college sports star at UCLA, he was that school's first four-letter man. During World War II Robinson served in the army as a lieutenant. In 1944 at Fort Hood, Texas, he was ordered by a white bus driver to sit at the back of the bus. Robinson refused, got into an argument with a white captain and was court-martialed for insubordination. He was acquitted, but the trial embarrassed the army and Robinson was honorably discharged.

The best job that the college-educated Robinson could find was playing baseball with the Kansas City Monarchs in the Negro Leagues. The Monarchs played him out of position at shortstop—Robinson did not have a shortstop's arm—but he could run and hit, and he established himself as a promising young player. Well before Branch Rickey, Wendell Smith picked him as the young player most likely to become the first to cross the baseball color line. In addition to the 1945 tryout with the Red Sox, Robinson worked out for White Sox manager Jimmy Dykes in 1946.

When he entered organized baseball, Jackie Robinson brought with him the aggressive, running-oriented Negro League style of play. "His bunts, his steals, and his fake bunts and fake steals humiliated a legion of visiting players," wrote sportswriter Roger Kahn. Displaying what Rickey called his "sense of adventure," Robinson stole home with a frequency not seen in the major leagues since the 1910s and made Houdini-like escapes from rundowns. His dar-

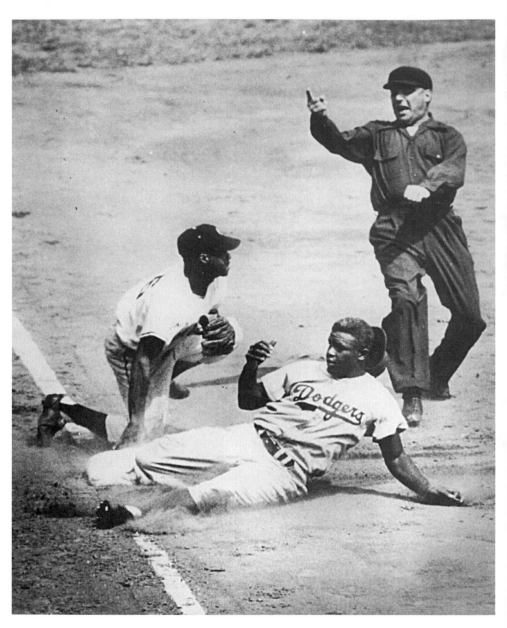

Jackie Robinson slides into third base. Robinson was the real hero of the breaking of the color line.

ing was all the more impressive because of the unimaginable pressure and loneliness of his early years in organized baseball. In 1949, his finest season, he scored 122 runs; drove in 124; and led the league in stolen bases, with 37, and in batting, at .342.

Nineteen forty-nine was also the year that Branch Rickey released Robinson from his promise to turn the other cheek. After that, the National League saw the real Jackie Robinson. In 1947 he had endured all sorts of racist heckling from the Phillies and their manager Ben Chapman without answering back; Robinson even posed for a photograph shaking Chapman's hand. When Chapman started in on Robinson again in 1949, however, Robinson answered: "You son of a bitch, if you open your mouth one more time I'm gonna kick the —— out of you." The press was not happy with the change. As Robinson put it in his 1972 book, *I Never Had It Made:*

> *I learned that as long as I appeared to ignore insult and injury, I was a martyred hero to a lot of people who seemed to have sympathy for the underdog. But the minute I began to answer, to argue, to protest—the minute I began to sound off I became a swellhead, a wise guy, an "uppity" nigger. When a white player did it, he had spirit. When a black player did it, he was "ungrateful," an upstart, a sorehead. It was hard to believe the prejudice I saw emerging among people who had seemed friendly toward me before I began to speak my mind. I became, in their minds and in their columns, a "pop-off," a "troublemaker," a "rabble-rouser." It was apparent I was a fine guy until "success went to his head," until I began to "change."*

Reporter Dick Young complained that when he was with Campanella or some of the other African Americans on the Dodgers he could forget about race, but that Robinson never let him forget the color of his skin. Hearing this, Robinson laughed and said, "Did it occur to you that I don't want Dick Young to forget?"

Jackie Robinson always remained close to Branch Rickey. He was disappointed when Rickey left the Dodgers, and after new Dodgers owner Walter O'Malley tried to trade him to the New York Giants in 1956, Robinson retired. After being elected to the Hall of Fame, in 1962, Robinson continued to lead a public life, campaigning with Martin Luther King and speaking out about civil rights. He was not forgotten by the African-American players who followed him across the color line. Don Newcombe said: "Through baseball, Jackie did more to tear down segregation in hotels and sports arenas than any other man. Nobody will ever do more, because it won't be necessary again." Willie Mays was more succinct. "Every time I look at my pocketbook," Mays said, "I see Jackie Robinson."

At the 1972 World Series Robinson criticized baseball for taking so long to finish the job of integration. "Someday," he said, "I'd like to be able to look over at third base and see a black man managing the ball club." Nine days later, at fifty-three, he was dead of a heart attack. Old friend Pee Wee Reese felt that part of the reason for Robinson's early death was the strain of having been the first to cross the baseball color line. "I don't think Jack ever stopped carrying the burden," Reese said. "I'm no doctor, but I'm sure it cut his life short."

THEY NEVER HAD IT MADE

From 1947 to Today

The courage, determination, and skill of Jackie
Robinson were an inspiration to the baseball world
and to all of America. Not too long after Robinson's
success in Brooklyn, the Cleveland Indians signed
Larry Doby as the first African-American player in
the American League. Dozens of all-white minor
leagues began to integrate or, in the case of some of
the older leagues, to reintegrate. The national gov-
erning body of amateur baseball announced that it
would allow interracial tournaments and leagues.
All-white professional football had signed four
African-American players in 1946, and other sports
broke their color lines. It is a testament to how much
the integration of baseball overshadowed that of the
other sports, that few fans today could tell you the
names of the first African Americans in football, bas-
ketball, golf, or tennis. Jackie Robinson's impact is
still felt, even outside the world of sports, and his
name is as well known today as it was in 1947.

In a sense, however, Robinson's crossing of the
color line was only the first step on the road toward

complete integration and racial equality in organized baseball. In the decades since 1947, this journey has proceeded painfully slowly.

By 1949 only eleven African-American players had been signed by major league teams, eight of them by the Brooklyn Dodgers and Bill Veeck's Cleveland Indians. Five major league teams—the Pirates, the Cardinals, the Reds, the Senators, and the Yankees—waited until 1954 to sign their first African American. Last and least were the Phillies (1957), the Tigers (1958), and the Red Sox (1959). For the decade of the 1950s only eight percent of all major league players were African-American or dark-skinned Hispanic. According to baseball writer Bill James, more Polish Americans were in major league baseball in the 1950s than African Americans.

Baseball was also slow to fight segregation in its own backyard. For years major league teams passively complied with Jim Crow laws and customs in the small Southern towns in which the majority of them held spring training or had farm clubs. As a result, African-American players were subjected to the humiliation of playing in ballparks with Jim Crow stands and being separated from white teammates at team restaurants and hotels. Baseball and baseball-related tourism was such an important source of income for these towns, however, that few of them could have afforded to continue their Jim Crow practices if baseball had insisted that they change.

Sometimes, major league clubs allowed their African-American ball players to be treated this way out of simple thoughtlessness. Many white players from the 1950s or even 1960s admit that they did not know where their African-American teammates slept or ate during spring training or in southern minor league towns; they never thought about it. Not that all of these problems happened in the Deep South. In his autobiography, former Tigers slugger Hank Greenberg recalled an event from his days as Cleveland Indians general manager. He had accompanied the Indians on a 1955 road trip to Baltimore, Maryland:

> *When we arrived at the Lord Baltimore Hotel all the players rushed to get off the bus . . . I found myself standing there with five black players. They were not going to the hotel because they were black. It hadn't occurred to me that these players would not be admitted into the hotel. I asked them "What do you guys do?" They said, "We wait for a taxi and this taxi takes us to different homes, different families in Baltimore, and we stay with them." I thought to myself, this is terrible. Here these fellows are a vital part of the team and contributing greatly to the success of the team, and they have to be segregated. . . .*[1]

Presumably, this had been going on since Larry Doby joined the Indians, in 1948. Greenberg discovered that African Americans were also not permitted in the team hotels in St. Louis or Washington, D.C. He soon learned, however, that green can sometimes be a more important color than black or white. When Greenberg wrote to the hotels, telling them that they would have to accept his entire team or lose the Indians' business, all of them chose to drop their Jim Crow policies.

Baseball signed many more African-American players in the 1960s and 1970s. During those decades the game was dominated by such African-American stars as Elston Howard, Willie McCovey, Maury Wills, Frank Robinson, Willie Mays, Hank Aaron, Bob Gibson, Willie Stargell, Joe Morgan, Jim Rice, and

Pittsburgh Pirate Roberto Clemente, the pride of Puerto Rico, was killed in a plane crash while on a mercy mission to Nicaragua.

Reggie Jackson. Most of these players didn't come from the Negro Leagues but were scouted, signed, and developed in the minors. On the surface, baseball seems to have welcomed the African-American athlete. Today, African-American stars are paid at least as well as their white counterparts. The percentage of African Americans in baseball is twice that in the general population.

But subtler patterns of discrimination and prejudice that evolved in the 1940s and 1950s have persisted. Statistics show that the average African-American player has always produced a little better than the average white player. This means that at some level in the scouting process or in the minors, mediocre African Americans do not get the same chance as mediocre whites. Like Frank Grant, Bud Fowler, and Fleet Walker, today's African-American players have to be a little bit better than white players to make it in baseball.

African-American players are also much more likely to play in the outfield or at first base (two positions that are closely linked; most first basemen are aging former outfielders). The reason for this may be that baseball scouts, coaches, and executives, who are overwhelmingly white, believe in the racial stereotype that African Americans are inherently faster than whites. As a result, they look for, and find, only fast African-American athletes. The flip side of this is that very few African Americans are put at important positions such as pitcher, catcher, and shortstop, which require little speed. In 1968 one study showed that only 13 of the 207 pitchers in the majors were African American. Another found that as recently as 1986, 82 percent of African Americans in the majors were outfielders or first basemen and 5.7 percent were pitchers. There were no African-American catchers in the 1986 study.

Anyone who thought that racism in baseball was a thing of the past found out differently on April 6, 1987. On that day the Dodgers general manager Al Campanis appeared on a television program commemorating the fortieth anniversary of Jackie Robinson's first game in the major leagues. Campanis had played with Robinson at Montreal in 1946 and was one of the first white players there to extend him a helping hand. When asked whether racial prejudice was the reason more African Americans were not hired as coaches, managers, and front office executives, Campanis shocked the country by answering: "No, I don't believe it's prejudice. I truly believe that they may not have some of the necessities to be, let's say, a field manager, or perhaps a general manager." He went on to say that "blacks are gifted with great musculature and various other things, and they're fleet of foot, and this is why there are a lot of black major league baseball players. Now, as far as having the background to become club presidents, or presidents of a bank, I don't know." Campanis's remarks were quickly disavowed by the baseball establishment, and Campanis lost his job. A few years later, baseball was embarrassed again when the owner of the Reds, Marge Schott, was quoted as using the word "nigger" at business meetings and making racist remarks about some of her own ball players. When this caused a public scandal, the other owners suspended Schott and forced her to undergo racial sensitivity training.

According to baseball, the racist remarks by Schott and Campanis are isolated cases. But many have wondered how atypical they really are. As did Albert Spalding, with his unusually open acknowledgment of racial prejudice in the 1860s, did Schott and Campanis actually give us a glimpse into the real thinking of baseball's owners and top executives?

Perhaps the best way to answer that question is to look at the major league baseball owners' hiring record. Jackie Robinson, the first African American to cross the color line in the twentieth century, reached the majors in 1947. Since the civil rights movement of the 1960s, however, the firsts have been few and far between. The first African-American umpire, Emmett Ashford, was hired in 1966. The first African-American manager, Frank Robinson, came in 1975. The first African-American league president was Bill White, in 1989. There has never been an African-American club president or general manager.

The color line on the playing field was broken almost fifty years ago. Jackie Robinson, Hank Aaron, Roberto Clemente, and Willie Mays have come and gone; the baseball Hall of Fame has opened up to African Americans, including some of the great Negro League stars of the past. But African Americans have been shut out of the top executive positions, where the business of baseball is run. Why has baseball been so slow to change? The answer may have something to do with another color line, one that has kept a part of baseball—ownership—as white in the 1990s as it was back in the 1870s, when professional baseball was born. Until this color line is finally broken, the process begun by Jackie Robinson may never be completely finished.

APPENDIX

PROFESSIONAL BASEBALL LEAGUES CHRONOLOGY

1845	New York Knickerbockers, first baseball club, is founded.
1858	National Association of Base Ball Players (NABBP), first organization of baseball clubs (amateur), is established.
1871	National Association (NA), first professional league, is formed.
1876	NA disbands; National League (NL) takes its place as sole major league.
1877	First three minor leagues are formed.
1880s and 1890s	Dozens of other minor leagues spring up.
1882	American Association (AA) becomes second major league.
1883	Tri-partite, or National, Agreement, clarifies major league–minor league distinction.
1884	Third major league, Union Association, lasts one season.
1890	Players' League, a player-owned cooperative major league, lasts one season.
1891	AA disbands, leaving NL as sole major league.

1901	American League (AL) founded; National Association of Professional Baseball Leagues, still the minor leagues' governing body, is formed and sets classifications for minors—A, B, C, D, now AAA, AA, A, Rookie.
1903	Present two-league, World Series format is established.
1914–15	A third major league, the Federal League, lasts two seasons.
1920	Negro National League (NNL) is formed.
1923	Eastern Colored League formed, lasts until 1927.
1929	American Negro League (ANL) lasts one season.
1937	Negro American League (NAL) is formed.
1930s–today	Led by Branch Rickey's St. Louis Cardinals, major league teams convert independent minor leagues into "farm systems."
1950s	With racial integration of the major leagues, the Negro Leagues are gradually forced out of business.

SOURCE NOTES

Chapter 1

1. Albert Spalding, America's National Game, revised and reedited by Sam Coombs and Bob West (San Francisco: Halo Books, 1991), 65.
2. George B. Kirsch, *The Creation of American Team Sports* (Urbana and Chicago: University of Illinois Press, 1989), 16.
3. Harold Seymour, *Baseball: The People's Game* (New York: Oxford University Press, 1990), 538.
4. Preston D. Orem, Baseball (1845–1881) from the Newspaper *Accounts* (Altadena, Calif.: self-published, 1990), 99.
5. Spalding, 82.

Chapter 2

1. *The National Pastime,* vol. 2, number 1 (SABR: 1983), 19.
2. Solomon White, *Sol White's Official Baseball Guide* (Philadelphia: Walter Schlichter, 1907), 17.

3.C. Vann Woodward, *The Strange Career of Jim Crow,* 3rd rev. ed. (New York: Oxford University Press, 1979), 43.

4. Lee Allen, *Hot Stove League* (New York: A.S. Barnes and Company, 1950), 31.

5.*The National Pastime,* 18.

Chapter 3

1. Irving Leitner, *Baseball: Diamond in the Rough* (New York: Criterion Books, 1972), 119.

2. Statistics on African-American players in nineteenth-century Organized Baseball based on Merl F. Kleinknecht in *Baseball Research Journal* (SABR: 1977), 118.

3. Robert Peterson, *Only the Ball Was White* (New York: McGraw Hill, 1970), 23.

4. *19th-Century Stars* (SABR: 1989), 131.

5. Peterson, 23.

6. Solomon White, *Sol White's Official Baseball Guide* (Philadelphia: Walter Schlichter, 1907), 83.

Chapter 4

1. Connie Mack, *My 66 Years in the Big Leagues* (Philadelphia: The John C. Winston Co., 1950), 6.

2. Jules Tygiel, *Baseball's Great Experiment* (New York: Oxford University Press, 1983), 14.

3. Solomon White, *Sol White's Official Baseball Guide* (Philadelphia: Walter Schlichter, 1907), 83.

4. Robert Peterson, *Only the Ball Was White* (New York: McGraw Hill, 1970), 31–32.

5. White, 87.

6. Richard Kluger, *Simple Justice* (New York: Alfred A. Knopf, 1976), 38.

7. C. Vann Woodward, *The Strange Career of Jim*

Crow, 3rd. rev. ed. (New York: Oxford University Press, 1979), 57.
8. *American Heritage* (April 1964), 102.
9. *Ibid.,* 103.

Chapter 5

1. Bill James, *The Bill James Historical Baseball Abstract* (New York: Villard Books, 1988), 101.
2. Lee Allen, *The American League Story* (New York: Hill and Wang, n.d.), 21.
3. Solomon White, *Sol White's Official Baseball Guide* (Philadelphia: Walter Schlichter, 1907), 83.
4. Robert Peterson, *Only the Ball Was White* (New York: McGraw Hill, 1970), 56.

Chapter 6

1. Jules Tygiel, *Baseball's Great Experiment* (New York: Oxford University Press), 1983.

Chapter 7

1. Jackie Robinson, *I Never Had It Made* (New York: G.P. Putnam's Sons, 1972), 92.

Chapter 8

1. Hank Greenberg, T*he Story of My Life* (New York: Times Books, 1989), 217.

GLOSSARY OF TEAM NAMES

N.B.: (1) Some teams from obscure minor or "outlaw" leagues, that is, white leagues outside organized baseball, are omitted. (2) Teams from different leagues or eras with the same name are not always the same franchise. For example, the NL Chicago White Stockings are the ancestors of today's Cubs; the AL Chicago White Sox are a different franchise that adopted the nickname the Cubs discarded.

KEY TO ABBREVIATIONS FOR LEAGUES

IND   Independent team, not affiliated with any league

Early Amateur League
NABBP National Association of Base Ball Players (1858)*

*year founded

Major Leagues

AA	American Association (1882)
AL	American League (1901)
FL	Federal League (1914)
NA	National Association (1871)
NL	National League (1876)
PL	Players' League (1890)
UA	Union Association (1884)

Minor Leagues

CSL	Connecticut State League (1884)
EInst	Eastern Interstate League (1890)
EL	Eastern League (1885)
IA	International Association (1877)
IL	International League (1884)
IntL	Interstate League (1880s)
KSL	Kansas State League (1887)
MSL	Michigan State League (1890)
MStL	Middle States League (1880s)
NE	New England League (1877)
NWL	Northwestern League (1895)
OIL	Oil and Iron League (1884)
OSL	Ohio State League (1886)
PCL	Pacific Coast League (1903)
SL	Southern League (1885)
WL	Western League (1879)

Negro Leagues

ANL	American Negro League (1929)
ECL	Eastern Colored League (1923)
LCBBC	League of Colored Base Ball Clubs (1887)
NAL	Negro American League (1937)
NNL	Negro National League (1920)
SLCB	Southern League of Colored Baseballists (1886)
USL	United States League (1940s): Branch Rickey's never-realized, white-owned Negro League

TEAMS

Acme Colored Giants (OIL): African-American; based in Celeron, New York

Adrian, Michigan (MSL)

Akron, Ohio (OSL)

All-American Black Tourists (IND): African-American

Ansonia, Connecticut (CSL): *see* Cuban Giants

Anson's Colts (IND): semipro team, not same as Chicago Colts (IND), or White Stockings (NL)

Atchison, Kansas (KSL)

Baltimore Orioles (NL)

Binghamton, New York (IL)

Boston Red Sox (AL)

Boston Red Stockings (NA, NL): ancestor of present Atlanta Braves

Brooklyn, New York (NL): ancestor of present-day Los Angeles Dodgers

Brooklyn Atlantics (NABBP, NA)

Brooklyn Brown Dodgers (USL): Branch Rickey's abortive attempt to form a Negro League club to play at Ebbets Field

Brooklyn Colored Unions (IND): early African-American club

Brooklyn Eckfords (NABBP, NA)

Brooklyn Excelsiors (NABBP)

Brooklyn Monitors (IND): early African-American club

Brooklyn Unknowns (IND): early African-American club

Buffalo, New York (IL)

Celeron, New York (OIL): African-American; *see* Acme Colored Giants

Chicago American Giants (IND, NNL): also known as Leland Giants

Chicago Columbia Giants (IND): African-American
Chicago White Sox (AL): ancestor of present White Sox
Chicago White Stockings (NA, NL): also known as Colts, Orphans; ancestor of present Chicago Cubs
Cincinnati Red Stockings (NA, NL): the first openly salaried team; ancestor of present Cincinnati Reds
Cleveland, Ohio (WL)
Cleveland Forest Cities (NA)
Cleveland Indians (AL)
Cuban Giants (IND, MStL, EInst, CSL): African-American, not Cuban
Cuban X-Giants (IND): African-American

Detroit Tigers (AL)

Fort Wayne, Indiana, Kekiongas (NA)

Homestead, Pennsylvania, Grays (ANL, NNL)
Houston Astros (NL)

Indianapolis Actives (NABBP)
Irvington, New Jersey, Irvingtons (NABBP)

Jersey City, New Jersey (EL)

Kansas City Monarchs (NNL, NAL)
Keokuk, Iowa (WL)

Leland Giants (IND, NNL) *see* Chicago American Giants
Louisville, Kentucky (AA)
Lynn, Massachusetts (IA, NE)

Memphis Eclipse (SLCB)
Meriden, Connecticut (EL)
Montreal Royals (IL): Brooklyn Dodgers farm team of the 1940s and 1950s

Morrisania Unions (NABBP): played in what is now the Bronx, in New York City

Newark, New Jersey, Little Giants (IL): later called Bears
New York Giants (NL): ancestor of present San Francisco Giants
New York Gorhams (LCBBC, MStL): African-American
New York Knickerbockers (NABBP): the first baseball club; founded by Alexander Cartwright and others in 1845
New York Mets (NL)
New York Mutuals (NABBP, NA)
New York Yankees (AL)

Oakland, California (PCL)
Oswego, New York (IL)

Page Fence Giants (IND): Bud Fowler's African-American club based in Adrian, Michigan
Philadelphia, Pennsylvania (MStL): *see* New York Gorhams
Philadelphia Athletics (NABBP, NA, NL): ancestor of present Phillies
Philadelphia Athletics (AL): ancestor of present Oakland A's
Philadelphia City Items (IND): sponsored by *City Item* newspaper
Philadelphia Giants (IND): African-American
Philadelphia Pythians (IND, LCBBC)
Pittsburgh Crawfords (NNL)
Pittsburgh Keystones (LCBBC, NNL)
Pittsburgh Pirates (NL)

Reading, Pennsylvania (InstL)
Richmond, Virginia (AA)
Rockford, Illinois, Forest Cities (NABBP, NA)

St. Louis Browns (AL): ancestor of present Baltimore Orioles

St. Louis Cardinals (NL)

Stillwater, Minnesota (NWL)

Syracuse, New York, Stars (IL)

Toledo, Ohio (NWL, AA)

Topeka, Kansas (WL)

Toronto, Ontario (IL)

Trenton, New Jersey (MStL): African-American, *see* Cuban Giants

Troy, New York, Haymakers (NABBP, NA)

Washington Alerts (IND): early African-American club

Washington Mutuals (IND): early African-American club; made up of federal government employees

Washington Olympics (NABBP, NA)

Washington Senators (AL): ancestor of present Minnesota Twins

Waterbury, Connecticut (EL)

Wheeling, West Virginia (OSL)

Worcester, Massachusetts (NE)

York, Pennsylvania (EInst): African-American, *see* Cuban Giants

BIBLIOGRAPHY

Alexander, Charles. *John McGraw.* New York: Viking, 1988.

Anson, Adrian Constantine. *A Ball Player's Career.* Mattituck, N.Y.: Amereon House, 1993. (Reprint of 1900 original.)

Barber, Red. *When All Hell Broke Loose in Baseball.* New York: DaCapo Press, 1982.

Holway, John. *Blackball Stars: Negro League Pioneers.* New York: Carroll and Graff, 1992.

Kluger, Richard. *Simple Justice.* New York: Alfred A. Knopf, 1976.

Oleksak, Michael, and Mary Adams Oleksak. *Beisbol: Latin Americans and the Grand Old Game.* Grand Rapids: Masters Press, 1991.

Parrott, Harold. *The Lords of Baseball.* New York: Praeger, 1976.

Peterson, Robert. *Only the Ball Was White.* New York: McGraw Hill, 1970.

Polner, Murray. *Branch Rickey: A Biography.* New York: Atheneum, 1982.

Robinson, Jackie. *I Never Had It Made*. New York: G.P. Putnam's Sons, 1972.

Seymour, Harold. *Baseball: The People's Game*. New York: Oxford University Press, 1990.

Tygiel, Jules. *Baseball's Great Experiment*. New York: Oxford University Press, 1983.

Veeck, Bill. *Veeck—as in Wreck*. New York: G.P. Putnam's Sons, 1962.

White, Solomon. *Sol. White's Official Baseball Guide*. Philadelphia: Walter Schlichter, 1907.

Woodward, C. Vann. *The Strange Career of Jim Crow*. New York: Oxford University Press, 1955.

Zoss, Joel, and John Bowman. *Diamonds in the Rough*. New York: Macmillan, 1989.

INDEX